what really counts
for students

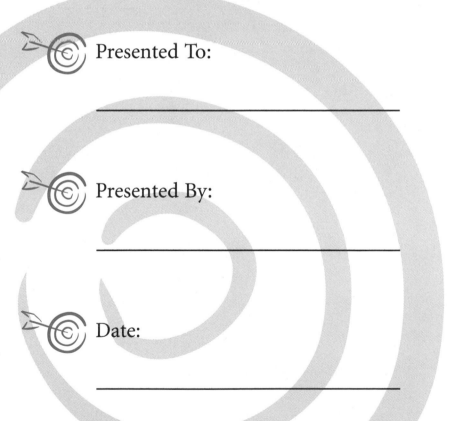

Presented To:

_____

Presented By:

_____

Date:

_____

what
really
counts
for students

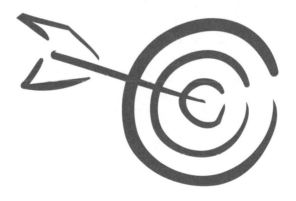

NELSON BOOKS
A Division of Thomas Nelson Publishers
Since 1798

www.thomasnelson.com

Published in Nashville, Tennessee, by Thomas Nelson, Inc.

Scripture quotations noted CEV are from THE CONTEMPORARY ENGLISH VERSION. © 1991 by the American Bible Society. Used by permission. • Scripture quotations noted GNT are from GOOD NEWS TRANSLATION, SECOND EDITION, copyright © 1992 by American Bible Society. Used by permission. All rights reserved. • Scripture quotations noted GOD'S WORD are from *GOD'S WORD*. *GOD'S WORD* is a copyrighted work of God's Word to the Nations Bible Society. Quotations are used by permission. Copyright 1995 by God's Word to the Nations Bible Society. All rights reserved. • Scripture quotations noted HCSB have been taken from the Holman Christian Standard Bible®, Copyright © 1999, 2000, 2002, 2003 by Holman Bible Publishers. Used by permission. Holman Christian Standard Bible®, Holman CSB® and HCSB® are federally registered trademarks of Holman Bible Publishers. • Scripture quotations noted MSG are from *The Message*. Copyright © by Eugene H. Peterson 1993, 1994, 1995. Used by permission of NavPress Publishing Group. • Scripture quotations noted NASB taken from the *NEW AMERICAN STANDARD BIBLE*®, © Copyright The Lockman Foundation 1960, 1962, 1963, 1968, 1971, 1972, 1973, 1975, 1977, 1995. Used by permission. • Scripture quotations noted NCV are from the Holy Bible, New Century Version, copyright © 1987, 1988, 1991 by Word Publishing, a division of Thomas Nelson, Inc. All rights reserved. Used by permission. • Scripture quotations noted NIV are from the HOLY BIBLE: NEW INTERNATIONAL VERSION®. Copyright © 1973, 1978, 1984 by International Bible Society. Used by permission of Zondervan Publishing House. All rights reserved. • Scripture quotations noted NKJV are from THE NEW KING JAMES VERSION. Copyright © 1979, 1980, 1982, Thomas Nelson, Inc., Publishers. • Scripture quotations noted NLT are from the *Holy Bible*, New Living Translation, copyright © 1996. Used by permission of Tyndale House Publishers, Inc., Wheaton, Illinois 60189. All rights reserved. • Scripture quotations noted NRSV are from the NEW REVISED STANDARD VERSION of the Bible. Copyright © 1989 by the Division of Christian Education of the National Council of The Churches of Christ in the U.S.A. All rights reserved.

Managing Editor: Lila Empson
Associate Editor: Kristen Lucas
Manuscript: J. Heyward Rogers
Design: Thatcher Design, Nashville, TN

Library of Congress Cataloging-in-Publication Data

What really counts for students.
    p. cm.
    ISBN 0-7852-0941-7 (pbk.)
    1. Students—Religious life. 2. Devotional exercises. I. Thomas Nelson Publishers.
    BV4531.3.W46 2005
    248.8'3—dc22

2005025134

Printed in the United States of America

05 06 07 08 09 QWK 5 4 3 2 1

Let us think about each other and help each other to show love and do good deeds.

HEBREWS 10:24 NCV

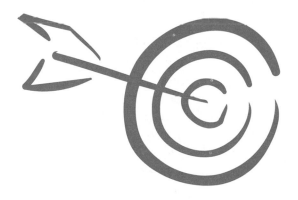

Contents

Introduction

**In Him we live and move
and have our being.**
ACTS 17:28 NKJV

Your life as a student is defined by due dates and deadlines—by the upcoming concert, the next big game, or next week's final exam. Add to that the demands of an active social life and worries about the uncertain future, and if you're not careful you'll find the urgencies—real and imagined—of your life have elbowed out the things that really count.

The things that really count don't always shout for your attention the way pop quizzes or the next round of the play-offs do. More often, the most important things whisper to you, quietly beckoning to you.

Love, prayer, friendship, character—these are some of the things that add up to a life of abundance and fullness, a life that surpasses mere busyness. It takes some effort to train yourself to attend to these things in the midst of so many other demands, but it's worth doing.

That's what this book is about. May you give yourself the time and perspective and will to gain the things that really count.

—J. Heyward Rogers

LIFE

An Introduction

> With You is the fountain of life; in Your light we see light.
>
> PSALM 36:9 NKJV

what really counts

From where you sit, life stretches out further than the eye can see. You have so many hopes, so many dreams, so many things you want to do and accomplish. You're so eager to get started, it's hard not to wish away the present. You want to be finished with school, be out on your own, get your career rolling, and maybe start a family. It seems forever before life gets going for real. For some people, that constant sense of waiting makes them feel that they're just killing time. When you have that attitude, there's little urgency motivating you to get serious about living for God.

You have to remember, however, that this earthly life is only the very beginning of your real life, your whole life. You are going to live forever. Even if your earthly life lasts a hundred years, it will still seem only a blink in the vast sweep of your eternal life.

But what an important blink it is! The decisions you make in this life will echo throughout eternity. It's vitally important that you invest the years and days and minutes you're given in such a way that they'll pay off in eternity. Are the things that take up your time and energy and resources really going to last? You may feel as if you have nothing but time. You can always get serious later about the things of God, right? No, the time is now. It's time to get serious about investing your life in what really counts.

If I live the life He gave me, God will turn it to His use.
BAYARD TAYLOR

Life
Getting Real

> Your real life is hidden with Christ in God.
>
> COLOSSIANS 3:3 NLT

what really counts

There's more to life than your present life on earth. It's important to remember that your life is eternal. What really counts are the things that last forever. The logic of heaven is often at odds with the logic of the world, and it's human nature to adjust your thinking to match up with the world you can see. But God calls you to use spiritual eyes to see the big picture and to include the eternal and invisible in your worldview. When you realize that this life is only the beginning, you can begin to live the good life that God has mapped out for you.

You've probably had a strange dream that seemed as real as life. It's funny how your mind tries to adjust to the twisted logic of the dream world. You don't stop to ask why you would have decided to do your class presentation in your underwear, or how a crocodile got into your kitchen, or why Spider-Man is your student body president. As long as you're in the dream, that's your reality. Then you wake up, and you laugh to think that you ever could have mistaken such weirdness for real life.

There's a sense in which your earthly life can be like one of those dreams. You constantly find yourself immersed in a logic that you know to be false. The movies say that sex should be casual. Advertisements tell you that things are more important than people. Magazines give the impression that you're too fat if you don't look like the people on their covers. You know that's not right when you take a step back and try to see the world as it must look from heaven. And yet the things of earth seem so real, so solid.

That's not to say your life on earth is less than real. But it's only a short episode in a larger life that's much more real, much weightier. Your earthly life is a tiny dot on the timeline of your eternal life. But because that tiny dot is all you can see with human eyes, sometimes it seems as if that's all there is. If you don't stay awake to the things of God, your mind tries to adjust to this world's logic. You conform to the immediately apparent reality, and your life looks less and less like the life God has in store for you.

Life
Getting Real

What Matters Most...

- Being in the world but not of it. You have a foot in two worlds.

- Staying awake to the things of God. The things you can't see are often more real than the things you can see.

- Knowing that the "good life" is a life spent in God's presence.

- Seeing the big picture. Spiritual farsightedness can save you a lot of heartache.

- Looking to the Scriptures to know what's important. The Bible is a reliable guide.

What **Doesn't** Matter...

- Earthly priorities. Your true priorities are set by God.

- Material values. The things that last aren't material.

- Superficial status symbols. In Christ you have incredible status.

- False idols. There is only one true God.

- Other people's opinions of you. You know who you are in Christ.

Focus Points...

We don't look at the troubles we can see right now; rather, we look forward to what we have not yet seen. For the troubles we see will soon be over, but the joys to come will last forever.
2 CORINTHIANS 4:18 NLT

Faith assures us of things we expect and convinces us of the existence of things we cannot see.
HEBREWS 11:1 GOD'S WORD

Lead me in the everlasting way.
PSALM 139:24 NASB

God has given us eternal life, and this life is in His Son.
1 JOHN 5:11 NKJV

The fear of the LORD leads to life, and he who has it will abide in satisfaction.
PROVERBS 19:23 NKJV

You will find as you look back upon your life that the moments when you have truly lived are the moments when you have done things in the spirit of love.

HENRY DRUMMOND

It is vanity to desire a long life and to take no heed of a good life.

THOMAS À KEMPIS

17

Life
Making It Count

> The earth and everything on it belong to the LORD. The world and its people belong to him.
> PSALM 24:1 CEV

what really counts

Once you begin to come to terms with eternity—that is, when you see your earthly existence as a speck on the timeline of eternal life—it may be tempting to view your earthly life as less important. Why study for final exams? On the vast canvas of eternity, isn't your grade in biology less than a tiny speck? Why play sports? Surely chasing a ball around a field has no eternal significance. Why spend any time with your friends? Wouldn't that time be better spent on something with more "eternal significance"?

That kind of thinking can get you confused very quickly. It ignores one simple fact: This is God's world. The earth belongs to God just as much as eternity does, and God has put you here to live for His glory. The kingdom of God doesn't exist only in heaven; it exists here too, and God's people are called to bring that kingdom to bear on all of human life. Professor Henry Zylstra put it this way: "Nothing matters but the Kingdom, but because of the Kingdom, everything matters."

God's domain is a lot bigger than the "spiritual realm." It's biology. It's sports. It's politics and family life and music, friendship and reading and church. It all belongs to Him. True, all of those things get corrupted. The healthy competition of sports can become win-at-any-price idolatry. Healthy friendships can degenerate into negative peer pressure and popularity contests. A love of learning can disintegrate into grade-grubbing and rote memorization. But that's all the more reason to take those good things seriously—to reclaim them for the kingdom of God. When they are done as unto the Lord, they matter very much: "Whatever you do, do it heartily, as to the Lord and not to men" (Colossians 3:23 NKJV).

Most likely you have many years ahead of you. Make that time count. Use it to grow the kingdom of God. You do that by offering up everything you have and do to the service of God. Ask, "How can I use this possession, this talent, this activity or event to show people what God is like?" Real spirituality isn't about retreating from the world. It isn't about doing fewer and fewer things. It's about doing more and more things for the glory of God. Nothing matters but the kingdom. But because of the kingdom, everything matters.

Life
Making It Count

What Matters Most...

- ◎ Real knowledge. All truth is God's truth.

- ◎ Real love. Love people.

- ◎ Real purpose. Life is about growing God's kingdom.

- ◎ Real abundance. A full life draws others to the One who came to give abundant life.

- ◎ Real spirituality. The kind that transforms the world.

What **Doesn't** Matter...

- ◎ Grades. Love learning, and your grades will take care of themselves.

- ◎ Popularity. Love people, and let your social status take care of itself.

- ◎ Having the most stuff. God always provides what you need.

- ◎ Constant activity. Simplify to focus on what really counts.

- ◎ An undefeated record. Sometimes doing all things for God's glory includes losing graciously.

Focus Points...

I have come that they may have life, and have it to the full.
JOHN 10:10 NIV

See how hungry I am for your counsel; preserve my life through your righteous ways!
PSALM 119:40 MSG

A faithful man will abound with blessings.
PROVERBS 28:20 NKJV

To choose life is to love the LORD your God, obey him, and stay close to him.
DEUTERONOMY 30:20 NCV

We capture people's thoughts and make them obey Christ.
2 CORINTHIANS 10:5 CEV

what really counts

May you live all the days of your life.

JONATHAN SWIFT

To be always intending to make a new and better life but never to find time to set about it is as ... to put off eating and drinking and sleeping from one day to the next until you're dead.

OG MANDINO

What Matters Most to Me About
Life

Life is a journey toward your true home in heaven. And yet you're called to make the most of it. These questions will help you strike a balance between being heavenly minded and making a commitment to God's kingdom here on earth.

◎ *Even though your life may seem very normal and unremarkable, your eternal life is well under way. How does that realization change the way you think about life on earth?*

_____

_____

_____

_____

_____

_____

_____

_____

◎ *What is one area of life that you have always kept separate from your "spiritual" life? How can you begin to reclaim that area for the kingdom of God?*

_____

_____

_____

_____

_____

_____

_____

what
really
counts

◎ *The world constantly tries to press you into its mold. But the Word of God transforms you into something better. How does a Word-transformed life look different from a world-conformed life?*

_____

_____

_____

_____

_____

_____

_____

_____

◎ *Sometimes people define Christian morality in terms of what you shouldn't do. But what are the things that you will do or should do as a Christian that the world can't do or doesn't do?*

_____

_____

_____

_____

_____

_____

_____

_____

Life's a voyage that's
homeward bound.
HERMAN MELVILLE

GOD

An Introduction

> "We live in him. We walk in him. We are in him." Some of your own poets have said: "For we are his children."
>
> ACTS 17:28 NCV

what really counts

The throne room of the gods was a relatively common image in the art and literature of the idol-worshiping religions of the ancient Middle East. A god sat on a throne like an earthly king, and around him guardian angels served as a celestial bodyguard, shielding him with their wings. Isaiah 5 describes a similar scene. In a vision, the prophet Isaiah was ushered into the throne room of the true God. There he saw angels flying around the throne of God. But the all-powerful God needs no bodyguard. Those angels weren't shielding God. They were shielding their own faces from the overwhelming brightness of God's holiness and power.

24

That's the kind of God you serve. He shines so brightly that even angels can't bear to look on Him. The human imagination can't begin to imagine God's fullness. And yet He chooses to make Himself known to the human mind and heart. The purest good deeds look like a dark shadow beside His holiness, yet He invites His people to come into His presence.

God is the great mystery. Yet His self-description is the simplest statement imaginable: "I AM." He is. Before there was anything else, He was. When everything you see around you is gone, He still will be. He is the beginning from which everything came, and the end toward which everything is going. You'll never get your mind around God. But still He invites you to have a relationship with Him. He invites you into His throne room.

> I am graven on the palms of His hands. I am never out of His mind.
>
> J. I. PACKER

God
God the Creator

The heavens are yours and the earth is yours; everything in the world is yours—you created it all.

PSALM 89:11 NLT

what really counts

"In the beginning, God created the heavens and the earth. Now the earth was formless and empty, darkness covered the surface of the watery depths, and the Spirit of God was hovering over the surface of the waters" (Genesis 1:1–2 HCSB). It's an amazing thing to think about: From black nothingness, from utter disorder, a universe began to take shape at the sound of the Creator's voice: "Let there be . . ."

But that was a long time ago. What does creation have to do with your life? Creation isn't something that ended in the book of Genesis. God is always creating. He is always bringing order out of chaos, always bringing something good out of raw materials that don't appear to have much potential. "[God] is before all things, and in Him all things hold together" (Colossians 1:17 NASB). God isn't only the Creator. He is the Sustainer, too.

That should be good news to a student. Between class and

26

clubs and jobs, dating and friends and parents, things can seem pretty chaotic and disorderly for somebody at your stage of life. You may not know what you're going to do with the rest of your life. You may feel like a nothing. You may feel "formless and empty." God can speak into a life like that. He can make something good out of the pieces of your life, however chaotic they may seem to you.

The created world can teach you a lot about the God who created it. A thunderstorm speaks of His awe-inspiring power. A sunflower speaks of His beauty, His craftsmanship, His attention to detail. A finch sings of His creativity. A platypus shows His sense of humor. But the biblical account of creation teaches another important lesson: God the Creator stands outside His creation and is not subject to its laws. In the universe you live in, nothing can come from nothing. But in the creation, God created everything out of sheer nothingness. Try getting your mind around that. And if God can create a whole universe out of nothing, He can make something beautiful out of your life too. Sometimes it looks like your world is spinning into chaos, like it's physically impossible that your situation could get better. But "physically impossible" means nothing to the God who isn't subject to physical laws—indeed, who invented physical laws. Chaos is just raw material for God.

God
God the Creator

What Matters Most...

- God's creative power. He can bring order out of the most chaotic life.

- God's creative work. Look around; the earth declares His glory.

- God's creative problem solving. He'll surprise you.

- God's sustaining hand. He's constantly tending to the creation.

- Your creativity. It's one way the image of God expresses itself.

What **Doesn't** Matter...

- The feeling that everything's falling apart. God the Creator is God the Sustainer, too.

- The seeming impossibility of your problems. God created the universe out of nothing; He can help you untangle your mess.

- Feelings of despair. Maybe you can't see a solution, but God can.

- Dead ends. God can give you a fresh start.

- The seeming randomness of the world. God is still in control.

Focus Points...

Don't you know anything? Haven't you been listening? GOD doesn't come and go. God lasts. He's Creator of all you can see or imagine.
ISAIAH 40:28 MSG

God decided to give us life through the word of truth to make us his most important creatures.
JAMES 1:18 GOD'S WORD

Everything comes from the Lord. All things were made because of him and will return to him. Praise the Lord forever!
ROMANS 11:36 CEV

Ever since God created the world, his invisible qualities, both his eternal power and his divine nature, have been clearly seen; they are perceived in the things that God has made. So those people have no excuse at all!
ROMANS 1:20 GNT

what really counts

God is God. Because He is God, He is worthy of my trust and obedience. I will find rest nowhere but in His holy will, a will that is unspeakably beyond my largest notions of what He is up to.

ELISABETH ELLIOT

He who governed the world before I was born shall take care of it likewise when I am dead. My part is to improve the present moment.

JOHN WESLEY

29

God

God the Redeemer

> Is He not your Father, who bought you? Has He not made you and established you?
>
> DEUTERONOMY 32:6 NKJV

In ancient Israel, a person who had gotten into serious debt had the option of selling himself into temporary slavery to pay off the debt. Slavery is what they had instead of bankruptcy courts. The problem, of course, was that once a person was enslaved, he didn't usually have any way of buying himself out. Slavery wasn't the best-paying job, after all. Aside from working out the term of his slavery, the slave's best hope for freedom was a redeemer—a person, usually a relative, who was willing to pay off the debt and set the slave free.

The good news of the gospel starts out with bad news: You owe a debt that you cannot repay. You are enslaved by a sin-debt. That's a fact you must acknowledge before the gospel can do its work on you. And whereas the debt-slaves of ancient Israel submitted to a temporary slavery, your slavery is permanent. You can't work it off. You can't pay it off. Your only hope is a redeemer. That's where the good news starts.

God Himself is your Redeemer. He paid the price for your sin so that you might be set free. He loved the world so much that He gave His one and only Son so that anyone who believed in Him should live in freedom forever, not enslaved by sin.

Why would God do it? What do you have to offer Him? Nothing. How could you begin to make a case that you deserve to be bought out of slavery? You can't. God redeems His people for one reason only: out of sheer, unconditional love. The truth is, sometimes that kind of love is hard to accept; it's human nature to think God must have recognized some good thing in you that made Him want you on His team. But that's not the gospel. The gospel is simply this: God did for you what you couldn't have done for yourself in a million years.

God is love. And He delights to give His people what they most desire. What really counts to a person who's enslaved? Freedom. And yet a slave is in no position to lay hold of the thing he desires. God the Redeemer has paid your sin-ransom. Sin is a hard slave driver. But God's yoke is easy, and His burden is light. Thanks to your Redeemer, you are free to serve a better Master.

God
God the Redeemer

What Matters Most...

◉ God's riches. The God who bought your freedom makes you rich.

◉ God's love. Thankfully, His love doesn't depend on your goodness.

◉ Your freedom. You have been bought with a price, and now you're free.

◉ Your security. Your Redeemer holds you, even when your grip slips.

◉ Your hope. You have a lot to look forward to.

What Doesn't Matter...

◉ Your old sin. The debt is paid forever. Your slate is wiped clean.

◉ Your self-righteousness. You aren't good enough to pay your way out.

◉ Your self-sufficiency. It simply isn't enough. You need to trust God on this one.

◉ Your doubts. God's grace is sufficient for you.

◉ Your weakness. That's where God's strength is made perfect.

Focus Points...

Tell the Israelites, "I am the LORD ... I will rescue you with my powerful arm and with mighty acts of judgment."
EXODUS 6:6 GOD'S WORD

I know that my Redeemer lives, and that at the last he will stand upon the earth.
JOB 19:25 NRSV

You will know that it is I, the LORD, who saves you. You will know that the Powerful One of Jacob protects you.
ISAIAH 60:16 NCV

GOD is my strength, GOD is my song, and, yes! GOD is my salvation. This is the kind of God I have and I'm telling the world! This is the God of my father—I'm spreading the news far and wide!
EXODUS 15:2 MSG

what
really
counts

The LORD redeems the life of His servants, and all who take refuge in Him will not be punished.
PSALM 34:22 HCSB

The distinction between Christianity and all other systems of religion consists largely in this, that in these others men are found seeking after God, while Christianity is God seeking after men.

THOMAS ARNOLD

The best place any Christian can ever be in is to be totally destitute and totally dependent upon God, and know it.

ALAN REDPATH

God
God the King

> It is God who directs the lives of his creatures; everyone's life is in his power.
>
> JOB 12:10 GNT

what really counts

One of the hardest things about being a student is the fact that you're so close to adulthood and yet don't have the freedom to run your own life. Every time you check the mirror, you look a little more like an adult. You're taking on more responsibilities. Perhaps you're driving. Maybe you have a job. But you've still got people telling you what to do every day. You still aren't totally in charge of your own life.

Here's the good news: You'll never be totally in charge of your own life. Doesn't that sound like good news to you? It's very good news. God is in charge of your life, and He's infinitely more qualified than you are to run things. That's not to say, of course, that you won't be making your own decisions. You're making decisions every minute of every day, and as you grow into adulthood, you'll be making bigger and bigger decisions. But ultimately it's God who rules over your life, and God is all-loving, all-knowing, and all-powerful. He wants what's best for you, He knows what's best for you, and no power can keep Him from doing what's best for you. God is King of your life, and there has never been another king so loving.

The news gets even better. God isn't King over just you. Nor is His kingship even limited to Christians. God is King over everything. As an old catechism answer puts it, "He rules over me, the world, and Satan." That's right; God rules over the world, and Satan, too, regardless of the fact that they don't acknowledge His kingship. In the end, even Satan himself will have no choice but to recognize that God rules over him. What does that have to do with you? Everything. Your King has plans for you—plans to use you to grow His kingdom. And not even the whole world, not even Satan himself, can thwart God's plans.

If you're like most people, you want to run your own life. But God offers you something even better: He offers the chance to serve the King of heaven, to follow the call of His purpose in your life. And, as you may know already, "all things work together for good to those who love God, to those who are the called according to His purpose" (Romans 8:28 NKJV). That's not a bad trade.

God
God the King

What Matters Most...

- ◎ God's love. He wants what's best for you.

- ◎ God's omniscience. He knows what's best for you.

- ◎ God's omnipotence. He is able to accomplish what's best for you.

- ◎ God's wisdom. He always gives you what you need when you need it.

- ◎ God's faithfulness. He never fails. You can know without doubt that He is always with you.

What Doesn't Matter...

- ◎ Your desire for self-rule. Rest in the rule of the God who loves you.

- ◎ Your rights. Serving God often means giving up your rights for the sake of something better.

- ◎ Your plans. You may plan your way, but God directs your steps.

- ◎ The success of the ungodly. God is still in control. Those who are ungodly will fail.

- ◎ The seeming failure of the godly. God is still King. Those who are godly will succeed.

Focus Points...

I know, O LORD, that a man's life is not his own; it is not for man to direct his steps.
JEREMIAH 10:23 NIV

Good leadership is a channel of water controlled by God; he directs it to whatever ends he chooses.
PROVERBS 21:1 MSG

You alone are God of all the kingdoms of the world.
2 KINGS 19:15 GOD'S WORD

Whatever the LORD pleases, He does, in heaven and in earth, in the seas and in all deeps.
PSALM 135:6 NASB

Many are the plans in a man's heart, but it is the LORD's purpose that prevails.
PROVERBS 19:21 NIV

what really counts

Dependence upon God makes heroes of ordinary people like you and me!

BRUCE WILKINSON

If the God you worship isn't sovereign, you'd better find the One who is—because you're going to need him someday.

ROY CARTER

God
God the Father

To all who received him, to those who believed in his name, he gave the right to become children of God.

JOHN 1:12 NIV

"Our Father, which art in heaven." What does that really mean? It means that God relates to His people as a father relates to his children. His every action toward you is motivated by love—even those actions that don't feel like love at the time. The heart of Christianity is the truth that God the Father adopts sinners into His family as His daughters and sons. You have all the rights, all the privileges, all the security of natural-born sons and daughters. You have the right to inherit God's riches. You have the security of a father's love. You have God's fatherly provision for your needs. You have His name. And as you grow, you look more and more like Him.

As J. I. Packer put it, God the Father loves His adopted sons and daughters just as He loves Jesus, His only begotten Son. Once a child is adopted, there is no legal distinction between that child and a natural-born child. And an adopted child can't be un-adopted. That's the kind of security you have with your heavenly Father. If you are in Christ, you can rest in the loving arms of a Father who has called you His own.

For a child who has been adopted, a whole new world unfolds before him. He didn't have much hope, but now he has a hope and a future. Consider what Paul said to the Christians at Rome: "You did not receive a spirit of slavery to fall back into fear, but you have received a spirit of adoption. When we cry, 'Abba! Father!' it is that very Spirit bearing witness with our spirit that we are children of God" (Romans 8:15–16 NRSV). That word *Abba* means "Daddy." When God adopts you into His family, it isn't a legal formality. He loves you, and He invites you to call Him Daddy.

Maybe you don't have a great relationship with your earthly father. Maybe you don't know your earthly father. Whatever your relationship with your father is like, know that you have a perfect Father in heaven. It's an amazing love that caused the Creator of heaven and earth to draw you into His family and declare you to be His child. You are the heir of God's riches, sharing in the inheritance of Jesus Christ Himself! That kind of relationship leaves no room for fear and doubt. Adoption opens a life of freedom and joy.

God
God the Father

What Matters Most...

◎ Your model parent. The more you mature, the more you look like your Father.

◎ God's provision. Your heavenly Father always meets your needs.

◎ Your training. God disciplines His children to make them what they were born to be.

◎ Your brothers and sisters. It's a big family.

◎ Your inheritance. The riches of heaven are yours.

What **Doesn't** Matter...

◎ Doubts about your standing before God. Adoption is permanent.

◎ Loneliness. God sets the lonely in families—and in the family of God.

◎ Your past. To be adopted is to have a fresh start.

◎ Problems with your earthly family. God the Father is also God the Healer.

◎ Feeling unworthy. Your worthiness isn't the issue. The issue is the grace of a God who desires to have you as a son or daughter.

Focus Points...

The Lord Almighty says, "I will be your Father, and you will be my sons and daughters."
2 CORINTHIANS 6:18 GOD'S WORD

You should behave . . . like God's very own children, adopted into his family—calling him "Father, dear Father."
ROMANS 8:15 NLT

I will declare the decree: The LORD has said to Me, "You are My Son, today I have begotten You."
PSALM 2:7 NKJV

All who win the victory will be given these blessings. I will be their God, and they will be my people.
REVELATION 21:7 CEV

The Spirit Himself testifies with our spirit that we are children of God, and if children, heirs also, heirs of God and fellow heirs with Christ, if indeed we suffer with Him so that we may also be glorified with Him.
ROMANS 8:16–17 NASB

What is a Christian? The question can be answered in many ways, but the richest answer I know is that a Christian is one who has God as Father.

J. I. PACKER

God loves each of us as if there were only one of us.
SAINT AUGUSTINE

What Matters Most to Me About
God

There's no getting your mind around God. He's God, after all, and you're only human. Nevertheless, time spent pondering God's character is time well spent. These questions might get you started:

◎ *God creates order out of chaos. How has God shown His creative power in your life? How has He created good things where before there had been only disorder and emptiness?*

_____

_____

_____

_____

_____

_____

_____

◎ *God buys His people out of their slavery to sin. How have you been set free from the bondage of sin? Are there areas of your life where you still feel bound?*

_____

_____

_____

_____

_____

_____

_____

what
really
counts

◎ *God is King over all. Is God's kingship over your life something you gladly embrace, or is it an idea that you resist? Why?*

_____

_____

_____

_____

_____

_____

_____

_____

◎ *God is Father to His people. A father performs many roles in the lives of his children. What aspects of God's fatherhood mean the most in your life right now?*

_____

_____

_____

_____

_____

_____

_____

_____

_____

There will be two kinds of people in the end: Those that will say to God "Thy will be done" and those to whom God will say "My will be done."

C. S. LEWIS

JESUS

An Introduction

> Whoever has the Son, has life; whoever rejects the Son, rejects life.
>
> 1 JOHN 5:12 MSG

Jesus was a great man. But was He more than that? He claimed to be God. When a man makes that kind of statement, everything changes. As C. S. Lewis pointed out, when a man claims to be God, either he's a liar, he's a lunatic, or He really is God. He can't be *just* a great man. Jesus didn't leave that option open.

The life of Jesus served as more than just a good example. He lived the perfect life that His people couldn't live so that He could die a death that would pay for all their wrongs. He made a way to God, and you can follow Him on the path.

There may have been a greater miracle to Jesus' life than His perfection—a miracle that was even greater than His resurrection from the dead. After all,

He was fully God; you wouldn't expect an all-holy God to sin. For that matter, the immortal God couldn't very well stay dead. As J. I. Packer pointed out, once you accept the fact that Jesus was God in human form, His resurrection really isn't as surprising as His death. No, the real miracle of Christ's life is the fact that He came to earth at all. He laid aside all the glory and honor that He enjoyed in heaven and emptied Himself to become a lowly human being. All so He could suffer and die to save people who had already rejected Him. Now that's amazing grace!

If our greatest need had been information, God would have sent us an educator. If our greatest need had been technology, God would have sent us a scientist. If our greatest need had been money, God would have sent us an economist. But since our greatest need was forgiveness, God sent us a Savior.

ROY LESSIN

Jesus
Jesus Came Down

He gave up his place with God and made himself nothing. He was born to be a man and became like a servant.

PHILIPPIANS 2:7 NCV

what really counts

Pretend for a minute that you have the ability to transform yourself into an ant and back again. Now pretend that, for some reason, you desire to have fellowship with ants. And since ants can't come up to your level, you're going to have to go down to theirs. You give up all the rights, all the privileges, all the power of your humanness in order to become an ant and live among the other ants in the anthill. You make yourself a worker ant, a member of the lowliest of the ant tribes. When you were a human being, you could have smashed the whole colony with one well-placed boot. But here in the anthill, you slave away at the queen's behest. You suffer the bullying of the soldier ants. How long do you think you would let yourself be humiliated and browbeaten by other ants before you had enough and went back to being a human?

Two thousand years ago, an even more amazing transformation took place: God became a human being. God the Son, the almighty, all-knowing Maker of the universe, left the throne of heaven, laid aside His glory, and became a baby. By His word He spoke the whole world into existence, but He had to learn to talk, just like any other baby. He had held galaxies in His hand, but He became as weak and helpless as any other baby. He went through puberty. He may have had pimples. At any moment He could have willed Himself back to heaven, but He didn't. The high King of heaven subjected Himself to every humiliation that goes with being a human being.

The apostle Paul put it this way: "You know the grace of our Lord Jesus Christ, that though He was rich, yet for your sake He became poor, so that you through His poverty might become rich" (2 Corinthians 8:9 NASB). You couldn't come up to His level, so Christ came down to yours. He emptied Himself of all the glory that was due Him. For your sake.

That's who Jesus Christ is. He is the God who loves you so much that He subjected Himself to every humiliation, every temptation, every heartache you'll ever live through. And now you are rich, for even as He shared in your humanity, He has allowed you to share in the riches of heaven. How much love is that?

Jesus
Jesus Came Down

What Matters Most...

◎ Boldness. Jesus loved you enough to set aside His heavenly glory for your sake. You have nothing to fear.

◎ Humility. At the same time, you are called to be like Jesus, who humbled Himself.

◎ Your spiritual wealth. Jesus made Himself poor in order to make you rich.

◎ Fellowship between you and Jesus. It was so important to Jesus that He came all the way down to your level.

◎ Jesus' glory. It's yours to share.

What **Doesn't** Matter...

◎ Obscurity. Even if you're just a blip on the world's radar screen, God knows your name and loves you enough that He sent His Son to redeem you.

◎ Self-sufficiency. The gospel is that God helps those who cannot help themselves.

◎ Feelings of worthlessness. Jesus thought enough of you to become a human being for your sake. That's all the worth you need.

◎ Self-importance. Jesus let go of His status; does any self-importance keep you from reaching out to other people?

◎ Humiliation. In your most humiliating moments, remember the humiliation that Jesus experienced for your sake.

Focus Points...

The Word became flesh and dwelt among us, and we beheld His glory, the glory as of the only begotten of the Father, full of grace and truth.
JOHN 1:14 NKJV

[Mary] gave birth to her firstborn son; and she wrapped Him in cloths, and laid Him in a manger, because there was no room for them in the inn.
LUKE 2:7 NASB

When the time arrived that was set by God the Father, God sent his Son, born among us of a woman, born under the conditions of the law so that he might redeem those of us who have been kidnapped by the law.
GALATIANS 4:4 MSG

Since the children have flesh and blood, he too shared in their humanity so that by his death he might destroy him who holds the power of death—that is, the devil.
HEBREWS 2:14 NIV

God came near. If he is who he says he is, there is no truth more worthy of your time.

MAX LUCADO

God's glory is best seen in Jesus Christ. He, the Light of the world, illuminates God's nature. Because of Jesus, we are no longer in the dark about what God is really like.

RICK WARREN

Jesus
Jesus Lived Among Us

Jesus wept.
JOHN 11:35 MSG

Jesus knows what it's like to be a human being. He lived the full range of human experiences, and yet somehow He remained sinless. That's what makes Him your perfect priest before God. Consider the scene when He raised Lazarus from the dead. Jesus wept. He stood beside the tomb and mourned with Mary and Martha, the dead man's sisters. He felt the same wrenching sorrow that they felt. The strange thing, of course, was that Jesus already knew how all this would end. Before He even made the trip to Lazarus's tomb in Bethany, Jesus had told His disciples that He would raise His friend from the dead. But in the meantime, He was shot through with the same sorrow that afflicted Lazarus's sisters. Then He called the dead man back to life, and the tragic scene was transformed into a scene of astonished joy.

Jesus could have raised Lazarus from the dead without taking on Martha's and Mary's emotions. He could have waved His hands, the dead man would have staggered out,

what really counts

and the sisters would have been perfectly satisfied. On to the next miracle. For that matter, He didn't even have to make the trip to Bethany. He could have done a long-distance healing and saved Himself the trouble. But He didn't. He entered into the inner world of the dead man's sisters. He understood them.

Do you feel misunderstood? It's an almost universal experience. Your parents never seem to have any clue what you're going through. Neither do your teachers or your bosses. Nobody who's supposed to be looking out for you knows what it's like to be you. You don't even understand yourself sometimes. But Jesus understands. It's part of the reason He came to earth and lived among His people—so He could understand what it's like to be a human being. He experienced the difficulties, the temptations, the joys—everything you experience.

Now Jesus is back in heaven with God the Father, and He's constantly putting in a good word for you, because He knows what you're going through. "We do not have a high priest who is unable to sympathize with our weaknesses, but One who has been tested in every way as we are, yet without sin" (Hebrews 4:15 HCSB). Therefore, you can come into the presence of God with boldness. The God who holds your life in His hands is able to sympathize with you in your struggles. He knows what it's like to be you.

Jesus
Jesus Lived Among Us

What Matters Most...

◎ Jesus' real-world experience. He chose not to distance Himself from any of the difficulties you experience.

◎ Jesus' advocacy on your behalf. He speaks on your behalf to God—because He knows firsthand what it's like to be a human being.

◎ Jesus' help in temptation. He's seen it all—though with better results than what anyone else experiences.

◎ Other people's feelings. Jesus showed compassion for the sufferings of others. He is your holy example.

What Doesn't Matter...

◎ Doubts. It's okay to ask questions of God, just as Mary and Martha questioned Jesus in their darkest hour.

◎ Feeling misunderstood. It's true that others won't always understand you. But Jesus always does.

◎ Temptation. Temptation is a test, not a sin. If you pass the test, good. If you fail, not so good.

◎ Self-pity. Empathy is in. Self-pity is out.

◎ Anything that would keep you from empathizing with a person in need. Jesus didn't have to empathize with you, but He did.

Focus Points...

Jesus grew both in height and in wisdom, and he was loved by God and by all who knew him.
LUKE 2:52 NLT

They told the woman, "We no longer have faith in Jesus just because of what you told us. We have heard him ourselves, and we are certain that he is the Savior of the world!"
JOHN 4:42 CEV

As he went ashore, he saw a great crowd; and he had compassion for them, because they were like sheep without a shepherd; and he began to teach them many things.
MARK 6:34 NRSV

When He went ashore, He saw a large crowd, and felt compassion for them and healed their sick.
MATTHEW 14:14 NASB

what really counts

[Jesus] is touched with a feeling of our infirmities, a sympathizing physician, tender and skillful; he knows how to deal with tempted sorrowful souls, because he has been himself sick of the same disease, not of sin, but of temptation and trouble of soul.

MATTHEW HENRY

Jesus was God spelling himself out in language humanity could understand.

S. D. GORDON

Jesus
Jesus Laid Down His Life

Christ also suffered for sins once for all, the righteous for the unrighteous, in order to bring you to God. He was put to death in the flesh, but made alive in the spirit.

1 PETER 3:18 NRSV

Jesus knew what lay ahead of Him. He spent the entire night in anguished prayer—prayer so intense that the very sweat on His forehead came out as beads of blood. In a few short hours, one of His own disciples would betray Him, and the soldiers would carry Him away. He would face a mock trial. He would be stripped and beaten and nailed to a cross. He would die. He prayed, "My Father, if it is possible, may this cup be taken from me. Yet not as I will, but as you will" (Matthew 26:39 NIV).

The Father didn't take the cup of suffering and death away from Jesus. There was no other way. The death that awaited Jesus wasn't an act of meaningless violence; it was the reason He had come to earth. It was a terrible thing, certainly; after all, it was the murder of an innocent man. But it was so much more than that. It was the ultimate act of love and self-sacrifice. It was the only sacrifice that could take

what really counts

away the sins of the world. The will of Jesus was to do the will of the Father. And the will of the Father was to save His people from their sins.

For centuries, the people of God had sacrificed animals to pay for sin. But none of those sacrifices were perfect or permanent. Year after year the Israelites made sacrifices, but they were never enough to wash away their sins. The best those sacrifices could do was to point the Israelites to the perfect sacrifice—the death of the perfect Lamb of God. The blood of bulls and goats, said the writer of Hebrews, was able to purify the flesh, but the blood of Jesus purifies your conscience and clears the way for you to serve the living God.

Jesus showed the right way to live. He set an example. He taught many good things. But that wasn't the ultimate reason He took on human flesh. Jesus didn't come to earth just so Sunday school teachers would have somebody to draw life lessons from. Here's what really counts about Jesus' perfect life: It made it possible for Him to die the perfect death. Jesus didn't just show the way for you to live; He made it possible for you to live. He was the Lamb of God, and through His perfect sacrifice He paid the sin-debt you couldn't pay.

Jesus
Jesus Laid Down His Life

What Matters Most...

◉ Receiving the love of Jesus. It is offered to you freely.

◉ Rejoicing in the love of Jesus. It is a reason to celebrate.

◉ Sharing the love of Jesus. It is something to tell others about.

◉ Christ's sacrifice. This is what all other sacrifices were pointing to.

◉ New life. Jesus died so that you might live.

What Doesn't Matter...

◉ Your inability to fully comprehend the love of Jesus. You'll never comprehend it; you can only receive it.

◉ Your old life. Christ's sacrifice makes you a new creature.

◉ Others' disbelief. Not everyone will accept Jesus' love. The question is: What will you do with it?

◉ Coldness of heart. Pray for a new passion for the God who loves you.

◉ The same old, same old. Just when you think the good news is old news, it surprises you with a new freshness.

Focus Points...

Christ had no sin, but God made him become sin so that in Christ we could become right with God.
2 CORINTHIANS 5:21 NCV

No one else can save us. Indeed, we can be saved only by the power of the one named Jesus and not by any other person.
ACTS 4:12 GOD'S WORD

By the power of the eternal Spirit, Christ offered himself to God as a perfect sacrifice for our sins.
HEBREWS 9:14 NLT

Walk in love, as Christ also has loved us and given Himself for us, an offering and a sacrifice to God for a sweet-smelling aroma.
EPHESIANS 5:2 NKJV

what really counts

Learn to know Christ and him crucified. Learn to sing to him, and say, "Lord Jesus, you are my righteousness, I am your sin. You have taken upon yourself what is mine and given me what is yours. You have become what you were not so that I might become what I was not."

MARTIN LUTHER

The joy of Jesus was his absolute self-surrender and self-sacrifice to his father—the joy of doing that which his father sent him to do.

OSWALD CHAMBERS

Jesus

Jesus Rose Again

> You don't have to wait for the End. I am, right now, Resurrection and Life. The one who believes in me, even though he or she dies, will live.
>
> JOHN 11:25 MSG

what really counts

It could have been the plot of a summer blockbuster. The general is captured in battle and thrown into a squalid prisoner-of-war camp. His captors gloat over him, certain that the war is won. What they don't know is that they never could have captured him in the first place if he hadn't let himself be captured. It is all part of the general's plan to destroy the prison camp and lead his captured soldiers to freedom. He knows the camp can't hold him. The guards aren't strong enough to keep him imprisoned any longer than he wants to stay. He plays it cool the first night. All through the second day he bides his time. Then, on the morning of the third day, he fights his way out, overcoming the guards, leaving the prison a shambles, leading his soldiers to freedom.

When Jesus conquered death, it was an inside job. He died so He could destroy death from the inside out. And when He did, He led His people from death into life. That's the resurrection: not just Christ's victory over death, but yours, too. Apart from the work of Christ, death lords it over the human race like a sneering class bully. But in Christ you can sneer back: "Death is swallowed up in victory. O death, where is your victory? O death, where is your sting?" (1 Corinthians 15:54–55 NASB).

In the movie *Big Fish*, the main character is a man who doesn't fear death. As a result, he lives a life of incredible courage. He's a risk-taker, and the risks he takes pay off in every aspect of his life. You can have that kind of courage too. When Jesus conquered death, He conquered fear along with it. If you don't fear death, what else is there to fear? The Resurrection means courage and hope—not just for the next life, but for this one, too.

The old preacher D. L. Moody once said, "Someday you will read in the papers that Moody is dead. Don't you believe a word of it. At that moment I shall be more alive than I am now." That's the kind of hope that fuels a courageous life. You've heard the saying "You can't get out of this life alive." Don't believe a word of it. When Jesus rose again, He raised you with Him. You can get out of this life alive.

Jesus
Jesus Rose Again

What Matters Most...

◎ The death of death. The grave couldn't hold Jesus—or anybody who trusts in Him.

◎ The life of Christ. He didn't rise to retire; He rose to rule, and He is ruling on your behalf.

◎ Your victory in Christ's victory. It's not just that Jesus conquers death; He takes you along for the ride.

◎ Your hope. The Resurrection means you have a lot to look forward to.

◎ Your joy. Christ conquered not only death, but the fear that steals your joy.

What Doesn't Matter...

◎ The fear of death. Jesus conquered death.

◎ The fear of anything else. If you aren't scared of death, what else do you have to be scared of?

◎ The denial of death. You're young, but it's not too soon to come to terms with the fact that this life isn't all there is.

◎ The apparent victory of evil. A risen Jesus will ultimately crush Satan.

◎ The opinions that some other people may hold. The life to come is real.

Focus Points...

God set him [Jesus] free from death and raised him to life. Death could not hold him in its power.
ACTS 2:24 CEV

In the same way that the Father raises the dead and creates life, so does the Son. The Son gives life to anyone he chooses.
JOHN 5:21 MSG

He will take these weak mortal bodies of ours and change them into glorious bodies like his own, using the same mighty power that he will use to conquer everything, everywhere.
PHILIPPIANS 3:21 NLT

what really counts

If the Spirit of Him who raised Jesus from the dead dwells in you, He who raised Christ from the dead will also give life to your mortal bodies through His Spirit who dwells in you.
ROMANS 8:11 NKJV

Christianity is a power religion. Christ has the power to re-create men from the inside out, as every man who has ever met Him knows.

PETER MARSHALL

What one sees depends on where one sets up one's shop. Mine is at the entrance of the empty tomb.

W. PAUL JONES

What Matters Most to Me About
Jesus

No life made so great an impact on human history as the life of Jesus. Spend some time thinking about His life, death, and resurrection.

⊙ *It's one of the great mysteries of Christianity: God the Son became a human being. Consider what that cost Him. Write some of your thoughts.*

_____

_____

_____

_____

_____

_____

_____

what
really
counts

_____

⊙ *What difference would it have made if Jesus had just done His miracles, lived His life, died His death, and risen again without bothering to live the full range of human emotions, temptations, and experiences?*

_____

_____

_____

_____

_____

_____

_____

_____

⊙ *The Bible says that believers die to Christ so that they might live with Him (see Romans 6:8; 2 Corinthians 4:10; 2 Timothy 2:11). What does that mean in your life?*

_____

_____

_____

_____

_____

_____

_____

_____

_____

⊙ *The apostle Paul said that if the Resurrection isn't a fact—if Jesus wasn't really raised from the dead—then the beliefs of Christianity are worthless, and Christians are of all men the most to be pitied. What do you think he meant by that?*

_____

_____

_____

_____

_____

_____

_____

_____

_____

_____

Jesus is honey in the mouth, music in the ear, a song of gladness in the heart.
SAINT BERNARD OF CLAIRVAUX

JESUS

THE HOLY SPIRIT

An Introduction

> Who among men knows the thoughts of a man except the man's spirit within him? In the same way no one knows the thoughts of God except the Spirit of God.
>
> 1 CORINTHIANS 2:11 NIV

Who is the Holy Spirit? He's one of the three persons of God, equal with God the Father and God the Son. He is a person who comes into the heart of a new believer the moment he accepts Christ as Lord. But God the Holy Spirit is different from Christ in that He doesn't have a human body. You can't see Him or touch Him as you could see and touch Jesus when God became flesh and walked the earth.

Since the Holy Spirit inspired all the people God used to write the Bible, He knows the mind of the Father and can also teach you how to apply Scripture to your life. It's impossible to do all the things God wants you to do without the power that comes from the Holy Spirit. You can ask Him to fill you every day to give you strength to live the Christian life. He is your comforter, who will be your friend and walk by your side when you need Him. He will convict you; He will prick your conscience concerning sinful thoughts, attitudes, or actions. He can make God's will known to you because the Bible says that "the Spirit searches all things, even the deep things of God" (1 Corinthians 2:10 NIV).

When you recognize Him and ask for His help, your life will be transformed in radical ways, and your family and friends will notice that there is something different about you. As author Steven James wrote, you will begin to "smell like God."

> One thing above all distinguishes me from a non-Christian, or from myself before I became a Christian: the indwelling life of Christ the Holy Spirit brings me.
>
> LARRY CHRISTENSON

The Holy Spirit
Real Power

I'll put my Spirit in you and make it possible for you to do what I tell you and live by my commands.

EZEKIEL 36:27 MSG

what really counts

Have you ever been at home during a storm when you lost power? First, the lights flicker, then *boom!* You're in complete darkness. For a while, it's fun—you get out the flashlights and candles, and you enjoy the peace. But after a while, the fun wears off when you realize you can't get online to do your homework or catch up with friends. Then the thought occurs to you that if the power doesn't come on by morning, you may have to skip your shower or go to school with shaggy, wet hair!

It's then that you really start to miss the power. You need an electrical source to keep up your normal life routine. It's the same way with your Christian walk. You can't live the way God wants you to without the Holy Spirit as your power source. Even if you go to church, read your Bible, and pray every day, you're not going to last forever on your own strength. After a while, you'll feel burned out.

God wants to energize you if you will plug into His Spirit. How do you do that? When you realize you can't do it on your own, confess your weakness to God and ask Him to release the power of the Holy Spirit within you. This means total surrender on your part. What if you don't know what to pray for, or you feel like your prayers are not going anywhere? That's not a problem. The Holy Spirit will take what you say and make sure God hears what you meant. Romans 8:26 says that "the Spirit helps us in our weakness. We do not know what we ought to pray for, but the Spirit himself intercedes for us with groans that words cannot express" (NIV).

As a Christian teen, you want your life to be radically different from your peers'. You want them to look at you and know you have a supernatural source for handling things. The easiest way to share your faith is when somebody asks, "Hey, what's different about you?" Not only can God's Spirit help you witness, He is there to give you strength to overcome everyday temptations and to love those who are downright unlovable. The Holy Spirit is your richest source of spiritual energy and can prevent you from burnout. His power is waiting for you to use. All you have to do is ask.

The Holy Spirit
Real Power

What Matters Most...

◎ The supernatural power of the Holy Spirit at work in the lives of ordinary people.

◎ A willingness to surrender to the Holy Spirit.

◎ A life that's transformed. That life is the work of the Holy Spirit.

◎ A life that shows forth God's glory. Only the Holy Spirit can do that.

◎ A life that counts. Rely on the Holy Spirit.

What Doesn't Matter...

◎ Doing it on your own. It takes the help of the Spirit to live the Christian life. Without it, you're headed for burnout.

◎ The tendency to think of the Spirit as an abstraction. He is as personal and real as God the Father or God the Son.

◎ Your strength or lack of it. The Spirit empowers and refreshes.

◎ Not knowing how to pray. The Spirit fills in the gaps for you.

◎ Going through the motions. Apart from the Holy Spirit, religious ritual isn't worth very much.

Focus Points...

May the God of hope fill you with all joy and peace in believing, that you may abound in hope by the power of the Holy Spirit.
ROMANS 15:13 NKJV

I will pour out my Spirit on every kind of people: Your sons will prophesy, also your daughters. Your old men will dream, your young men will see visions.
JOEL 2:28 MSG

Go and make disciples of all nations, baptizing them in the name of the Father and of the Son and of the Holy Spirit.
MATTHEW 28:19 NIV

The right words will be there. The Holy Spirit will give you the right words when the time comes.
LUKE 12:12 MSG

what really counts

Sometimes I feel so filled with the Holy Spirit that I'm going to bubble over. Other times I feel as if I'm here, and the Holy Spirit is in Argentina. But my being filled ... is not based on feelings.

JOSH MCDOWELL

Trying to do the Lord's work in your own strength is the most confusing, exhausting, and tedious of all work. But when you are filled with the Holy Spirit, then the ministry of Jesus just flows out of you.

CORRIE TEN BOOM

69

The Holy Spirit
Divine Friend

> I will ask the Father, and he will give you another Helper to be with you forever.
>
> JOHN 14:16 NCV

It happened at a dinner party. The guests, all close friends, reclined around a table enjoying roasted lamb, seasoned vegetables, and warm homemade bread. It was the evening before a favorite holiday, and the room was full of electricity and anticipation. As they ate, the leader of the group began to speak. He was a great storyteller and always knew how to capture their attention. But tonight His stories were different, a little sad, even. He went around the room washing His friends' dusty feet and told them He would be leaving them soon. They were a little confused, but He told them, "Don't let your hearts be troubled. Trust in God, and trust in me" (John 14:1 NCV).

Their leader, Jesus, loved His friends and didn't want them to be lonely after He left. He knew how sorrow would cut deep grooves in their hearts. He told them they would soon have another friend, a Counselor, who would be with them forever after He was gone. They would never be alone again because, Jesus told them, "the Holy Spirit . . . will teach you all things and will remind you of everything I have said to you" (John 14:26 NIV). After He left, the promised Counselor did come and comforted them and filled their hearts with hope.

The Holy Spirit empowered the disciples to overcome their fears and to teach boldly. The same Holy Spirit is always with you, too. Do you ever feel alone even when you're in a crowd? You can be surrounded by friends at a football game or at the mall, and still feel as if nobody really understands you. You might feel as if your parents are too busy or have forgotten what it's like to be a teen, and you feel as if there's nobody you can talk to. Maybe you've been hurt or disappointed by someone you cared about deeply.

But you're never alone if you believe what Jesus said to His closest friends. He has given His followers the Holy Spirit, who lives in you and can comfort you always. He is God the Friend, who walks by your side. And He's never more than a prayer or a Scripture away. When you pour out your heart to Him, He listens. "Be still," He says, "and know that I am God" (Psalm 46:10 NIV). Sometimes, the only time you're able to listen to Him is when you're alone.

The Holy Spirit
Divine Friend

What Matters Most...

- Believing the Holy Spirit is real and omniscient.

- Inviting Him to fill you so you can be empowered.

- Asking Him to illuminate your mind so you can understand the Bible and apply it to your life.

- Listening to His voice in your spiritual conscience so you can overcome temptation and do what is right.

- Thanking Him for comforting you when you feel alone.

What Doesn't Matter...

- Your feelings. Your authority is God's Word, not how you feel.

- Your own abilities. You can't live the Christian life without the strength of God's Spirit.

- Your knowledge. Your life won't be transformed by what you know; it will change when you obey God's voice in your daily decision making.

- A contrary belief system. No one can understand the spiritual realm without being guided by the Holy Spirit.

- Comparing God's work in your life to someone else's. Everyone grows spiritually at a different pace.

Focus Points...

O my Comforter in sorrow, my heart is faint within me.
JEREMIAH 8:18 NIV

Don't grieve God. Don't break his heart. His Holy Spirit, moving and breathing in you, is the most intimate part of your life, making you fit for himself.
EPHESIANS 4:30 MSG

Jesus, being filled with the Holy Spirit, returned from the Jordan and was led by the Spirit into the wilderness.
LUKE 4:1 NKJV

Do not quench the Spirit. Do not despise the words of prophets, but test everything; hold fast to what is good; abstain from every form of evil.
1 THESSALONIANS 5:19–22 NRSV

what really counts

Surely you know that you are God's temple and that God's Spirit lives in you!
1 CORINTHIANS 3:16 GNT

Spell this out in capital letters: THE HOLY SPIRIT IS A PERSON.

A. W. TOZER

When I find myself racing around, trying to fill a day with mindless tasks or petty entertainment, this is usually the time that God whispers to my heart to draw away with Him and to silence my heart as He wishes to speak.

K. WALDEN

What Matters Most to Me About
The Holy Spirit

When you confess Christ as your Savior and Lord, the Holy Spirit comes to live within you. Take a few minutes to reflect on what it means to be filled with the Holy Spirit.

◉ *Ask God to give you a desire to be filled with the Holy Spirit. Jesus said that "those who hunger and thirst for righteousness . . . will be filled" (Matthew 5:6 NIV). Write a prayer that will remind you of the moment you began praying to be filled with His Spirit.*

what really counts

_____

_____

_____

_____

_____

_____

_____

_____

◉ *Write about a time when the Holy Spirit brought comfort into your life.*

_____

_____

_____

_____

_____

_____

_____

⊙ *Pray to be filled with the Holy Spirit. Ephesians 5:18 reads, "Do not get drunk on wine, which leads to debauchery. Instead, be filled with the Spirit" (NIV). What steps can you take today to live in the power of God's Spirit?*

_____

_____

_____

_____

_____

_____

_____

⊙ *Don't depend on your feelings. Some days you'll feel so happy you will be naturally bubbling over with joy. Other days, you will wonder if God has forgotten about you. You can place your faith (trust) in the promises of God and His Word. Thank God for filling you with the Holy Spirit, and write down how you hope your life will change as a result of this process.*

_____

_____

_____

_____

_____

_____

_____

_____

Thank God for the glorious and majestic truth that his Spirit can work the very nature of Jesus into us, if we will only obey him.

OSWALD CHAMBERS

FAITH

An Introduction

> Faith is the substance of things hoped for, the evidence of things not seen.
>
> HEBREWS 11:1 NKJV

what really counts

There is more to faith than simply acknowledging that a set of facts is true. As the book of James says, even the demons believe that God exists, and they shudder at the thought (see James 2:19). That kind of belief doesn't do them any good. It doesn't do anybody any good. Real faith—saving faith—means taking God at His word. It means hearing what God has said and changing your life as a result of it. Saving faith filters through your whole life.

Faith isn't something you can check off a list: (1) I believe . . . Check. (2) I believe . . . Check. (3) I believe . . . Yep, I believe that, too. Faith means that your every choice is made in light of those truths that you believe and acknowledge. You believe that God rewards those who are a friend to the friendless. Do you believe it is enough to get up from your usual spot in the cafeteria and have lunch with someone who's lonely? You believe that God can forgive any sin, no matter how great. Do you believe it enough to let go of your past mistakes and start fresh in the new life God offers? Do you believe it is enough to forgive those who have wronged you?

The life of faith is a great adventure. You don't know where it's going to lead. But that's the point, isn't it? You don't know what God has in store, but you know He's perfectly faithful and that He rewards those who put their faith in Him.

Love is the crowning grace in Heaven, but faith is the conquering grace upon earth.

THOMAS WATSON

Faith

Faith Is a Journey

We live by faith, not by sight.

2 CORINTHIANS 5:7 NIV

what really counts

David Livingstone was a poor Scottish teenager working in a mill when he first heard of mission work going on in Africa. Though times were hard in the 1830s, he set his mind on becoming a medical missionary. After scraping up enough money to complete his education, he set sail for the great, unknown continent of Africa. He went places where no European had ever gone before, and he shared his great faith in God with the people he met. During his lifetime, he traveled thousands of miles and saw some incredible things, including the magnificent Victoria Falls.

No one had ever done what David Livingstone was doing. You might say he was making it up as he went along. But another way to look at it—a more accurate way—is to say that he was walking by faith and not by sight. He was letting God direct him on a journey, and he didn't worry about the fact that he didn't know the next step.

How about you? You may feel like you're ready to start exploring uncharted territory, but you're stuck in school and not really sure where you want to go. When you look around you, it seems as if everyone else has it together and knows what he wants to do and where he hopes to be in the next decade. That's where faith comes in. Your goal in life is not to get somewhere; your goal is to let God take you on His journey. As you walk by faith, you will begin to see where God wants you and what He wants you to do. But you can live that way only if you're ready to trust God more than you trust the things you see around you. And that means constantly turning to Him—every time you make a choice, every time you feel afraid, every time you're tempted to stray from the path.

Faith isn't a one-shot deal. You don't believe just once; you believe every day and every minute of every day. The Christian life is a journey, and every step is a step of faith. It just takes a little faith in a great God to accomplish the unbelievable. Jesus said, "If you have faith as small as a mustard seed, you can say to this mountain, 'Move from here to there' and it will move. Nothing will be impossible for you" (Matthew 17:20 NIV).

Faith
Faith Is a Journey

What Matters Most...

◎ Trusting God. He will take care of the big plans of your life.

◎ Taking small steps of faith. You'll get to your destination, slowly but surely.

◎ Reading your Bible every day. Keep your life heading in the right direction.

◎ Believing in what you can't see. It's just as real as what you can see.

◎ Placing your hope in God and not in your circumstances. After all, God made your circumstances.

What Doesn't Matter...

◎ Knowing the details of where God is taking you on His journey. He will direct your steps.

◎ Thinking that you're stuck at a dead end or on a detour that's going nowhere. God has a journey for you.

◎ Feelings of doubt. You'll feel doubt, but God is faithful.

◎ Comparing your journey of faith to those around you. Your journey is for you alone.

◎ The temptation to take matters into your own hands. God's path is the right path for you.

Focus Points...

Show me the path where I should walk, O Lord; point out the right road for me to follow.
PSALM 25:4 NLT

Your life is a journey you must travel with a deep consciousness of God. It cost God plenty to get you out of that dead-end, empty-headed life you grew up in.
1 PETER 1:17–18 MSG

Your statutes have been my songs in the house of my pilgrimage.
PSALM 119:54 NKJV

In all your ways acknowledge Him, and He will make your paths straight.
PROVERBS 3:6 NASB

what really counts

God makes people right with himself through their faith in Jesus Christ. This is true for all who believe in Christ, because all people are the same.
ROMANS 3:22 NCV

Faith is to believe what we do not see, and the reward of faith is to see what we believe.

SAINT AUGUSTINE

At the beginning of every act of faith, there is often a seed of fear. For great acts of faith are seldom born out of calm calculation.

MAX LUCADO

Faith
God Is Faithful

If we are faithless, He remains faithful; He cannot deny Himself.

2 TIMOTHY 2:13 NKJV

Abraham believed God, and God viewed that belief as righteousness (see Romans 4:3). Perhaps it's the most incredible truth in the Christian faith: Your right relationship with God doesn't come from what you do or how faithful or how trustworthy you are. Rather, it comes down to a single question: Do you believe that God is going to do what He says He's going to do? Abraham believed God. Sometimes he didn't live like a man who trusted that God was going to see him through. Sometimes he took matters into his own hands, and when he did, he made some very serious mistakes. But when he came to his senses, he found that God was always faithful, even when he had been faithless.

Salvation by faith alone is one of the central teachings of the Bible. But be aware of this: You aren't putting your faith in faith. You're putting your faith in God. Your faith is sometimes strong, sometimes weak. If you're putting your faith in your own ability to trust or believe, you are sure to get discouraged. But God is perfect. He doesn't lie. You can take Him at His word. Do you want a stronger faith? Meditate on the faithfulness of God.

There's a beautiful story in the Gospels about a man who brought his demon-possessed son to Jesus for healing. Jesus said, "All things are possible to him who believes." The man's answer to Jesus was incredibly honest: "I do believe. Help me in my unbelief" (see Mark 9). Jesus honored that kind of honesty—the honesty of a man who sincerely wanted to believe, but knew that his belief was far from perfect. The man didn't try to fake it. Instead he turned the whole matter over to the One who is always faithful. And Jesus healed the man's son. He looked at the man and saw not the weakness of his faith, but the strength of his desire.

If you want to see God's work in your life, you have to have faith. But how much faith is enough? Like every human being, you're imperfect. The strength of your faith will go up and down. But you can thank God that in the end the strength of your faith isn't nearly as important as the strength of the God you put your faith in. God is faithful—perfectly faithful—even when your faith is lacking.

Faith
God Is Faithful

What Matters Most...

- God's faithfulness. He always does what He says He will do.

- God's power. He can do all things.

- God's goodness. He delights to reward the faithful.

- Simple trust. It's enough to know that "I am weak, but He is strong."

- The willingness to ask. Bring your troubles to the God who heals.

What Doesn't Matter...

- Your faithlessness. Even when you're faithless, God is faithful.

- The seeming impossibility of your circumstances.

- Your weakness. God's strength is made perfect in weakness.

- Your challenges. All things are possible with God.

- Your waning confidence. Place your confidence in the unfailing God.

Focus Points...

You don't neeed a thing, you've got it all! All God's gifts are right in front of you ... God, who got you started in this spiritual adventure, shares with us the life of his Son and our Master Jesus. He will never give up on you.
1 CORINTHIANS 1:7–9 MSG

What if some did not believe? Will their unbelief make the faithfulness of God without effect?
ROMANS 3:3 NKJV

After Jesus went inside, the blind men went with him. He asked the men, "Do you believe that I can make you see again?" They answered, "Yes, Lord." Then Jesus touched their eyes and said, "Because you believe I can make you see again, it will happen." Then the men were able to see.
MATTHEW 9:28–30 NCV

what really counts

It is not great faith, but true faith, that saves; and the salvation lies, not in the faith, but in the Christ in whom faith trusts ... Surely a man can believe what he knows to be true; and as you know Jesus to be true, you, my friend, can believe in Him.

CHARLES SPURGEON

Faith is the art of holding on to things your reason has once accepted in spite of your changing moods.

C. S. LEWIS

What Matters Most to Me About
Faith

As you begin to trust God more with the plans for your life, you can almost enjoy losing that sense of control, since you know that He has you safe in His hands.

⊙ *When do you remember first placing your faith in God? Write down some details of what led you to make that decision.*

_____

_____

_____

_____

_____

_____

_____

_____

⊙ *Has your faith grown since that point? How can you make sure that your faith is being strengthened every day?*

_____

_____

_____

_____

_____

_____

_____

_____

Can you name a time when your faith was tested? Did this circumstance make you feel closer to God or farther away?

_____

_____

_____

_____

_____

_____

_____

_____

_____

In Psalm 17:6 David wrote, "I am praying to you because I know you will answer, O God. Bend down and listen as I pray" (NLT). How does this prayer demonstrate David's faith? Do you have faith like David's? Why or why not?

_____

_____

_____

_____

_____

_____

_____

_____

_____

_____

Blessed are those whose strength is in you,
who have set their hearts on pilgrimage.
PSALM 84:5 NIV

FAITH

LOVE

An Introduction

> Most of all, love each other as if your life depended on it. Love makes up for practically anything.
>
> 1 PETER 4:8 MSG

what really counts

Jesus said, "No one has greater love than this, to lay down one's life for one's friends" (John 15:13 NRSV). When He died on the cross, Jesus demonstrated what the greatest love of all really looks like. He loved you to death. But He isn't talking just about Himself when He speaks of a love that lays down its life. He's talking about anybody who would practice a Christlike love.

You probably won't be called upon to die for the people you love. But you will be called upon to stop living just for yourself. You will be called upon to lay aside your plans, your convenience, your comfort; you may even be called to give up your hopes of being part of the in crowd at school.

If that's the case, you may be wondering, "What's in it for me?" Jesus gives the answer: "Those who lose their life for my sake will find it" (Matthew 16:25 NRSV). What's in it for you? A full, happy life. Yes, self-sacrifice is a component of real love, but it's not the most important component. Love isn't about throwing your life away. It's about letting go of your self-serving agenda so you can grab hold of a better, more fulfilling life. A life lived without love curves in on itself until it's closed to any joy that might try to come in from the outside. Love straightens you out and opens you up to receive the blessings that God showers on those who live for something besides themselves.

> Love a man, even in his sin, for that love is a likeness of the divine love, and is the summit of love on earth.
> FYODOR DOSTOYEVSKY

Love
Refuse to Use

> Love each other with genuine affection, and take delight in honoring each other.
>
> ROMANS 12:10 NLT

The word *love* is used to mean a lot of different things, some of which are quite contradictory. When a mother says, "I love my child," she means something like, "I want what's best for my child; I'm willing to do whatever it takes to make sure my child's best interests are protected." On the other hand, when a person who's hunkered down behind a ten-piece bucket at KFC says, "I love chicken," she means something else entirely, something like, "I'm deriving pleasure from this chicken." But the chicken's best interest is the farthest thing from that person's mind.

Sometimes when a person says "I love you," he means nothing more than "I derive pleasure from you." But that's not loving. That's using. That kind of "love" has the potential to hurt the "loved" one if her best interests ever come into conflict with the pleasure of the lover. When a girlfriend wants a little space from her boyfriend, or a son needs to cut his mother's apron strings, or a friend wins an award that another friend wanted—that's when the nature of love is revealed. Real love actively seeks what's best for the loved one, even at the expense of its own gratification.

Real love means finding your own happiness in the happiness of another person. Or to put it another way, to love a person is to line up your own happiness with theirs. But be forewarned: It's a risky thing to do. When you open yourself up to another person, you can get hurt. When you love a person, his heartbreaks become yours. When you love somebody—really love him—you give up the right to check out when times get tough.

His last night on earth, Jesus commanded His disciples to love one another, and He gave them the reason why: "So that My joy may be in you, and that your joy may be made full" (John 15:11 NASB). In spite of the risks, loving others is really the only way to find joy. You can't live a full life without putting something on the line. Sure, you can seal yourself off. You can harden your heart. You can suck people dry without giving them anything in return. But don't expect much fulfillment from that kind of life. When you stop using people and start loving them, you realize that there's more joy in your relationships than you thought possible.

Love
Refuse to Use

What Matters Most...

◎ Opening yourself up to others. The rewards are worth any risk.

◎ Loosening your grip. How else will your hands be free to receive God's blessings?

◎ Seeking what's best for the people you love. In seeking their joy, you find your own.

◎ Pursuing the long-term joy of loving another person rather than the short-term gratification of using them.

◎ Sticking it out when a relationship faces challenges.

What Doesn't Matter...

◎ Your natural tendency to use people. That isn't love; that is its opposite.

◎ Your natural selfishness. It leads to loneliness and to hardness of heart.

◎ Your fear of rejection. God always accepts you.

◎ The impulse to force your agenda on the people you love. God's agenda is what matters, not yours.

◎ The risk of being hurt. The rewards far outweigh the risks.

Focus Points...

Let all that you do be done in love.
1 CORINTHIANS 16:14 NRSV

Love does no harm to a neighbor; therefore love is the fulfillment of the law.
ROMANS 13:10 NKJV

Beyond all these things put on love, which is the perfect bond of unity.
COLOSSIANS 3:14 NASB

The LORD shows mercy and is kind. He does not become angry quickly, and he has great love.
PSALM 103:8 NCV

If I give everything I own to the poor and even go to the stake to be burned as a martyr, but I don't love, I've gotten nowhere. So, no matter what I say, what I believe, and what I do, I'm bankrupt without love.
1 CORINTHIANS 13:3 MSG

**what
really
counts**

Against persistent love there is nothing that can be done; it blunts all weapons.

STUART MORRIS

Love is not affectionate feeling, but a steady wish for the loved person's ultimate good as far as it can be obtained.

C. S. LEWIS

Love
Because God Loves You

Your love means more than life to me, and I praise you.
PSALM 63:3 CEV

what really counts

"Love your enemies." That's an outrageous demand when you think about it. Love the backstabbing gossip? Love the school bully? It flies in the face of most people's concept of love. After all, you don't have much control over your feelings. But Jesus isn't talking about what you should or shouldn't feel. He's talking about what you should do. He's talking about your will. Jesus calls you to treat people—even people who consider you their enemy—the way He would treat them. That means not answering evil for evil, but rather giving back good. It means seeking what's best for others, even if they wish the worst on you. It's not the response that comes naturally. That's what makes it an act of the will.

Love is more than a response to another person's loveliness. Everybody loves the popular kids, the beautiful people. It's no great accomplishment to love a person who loves you back, or who makes you feel good about yourself. But to love somebody who hates you—or even somebody who just gets on your nerves—that's something special. Love shows what it's made of when it seeks the happiness of the unlovable. That's true godliness.

Where do you find the will to love your peers, your siblings, your teachers, and your parents that way? You love because God loved you first. It helps to remember that God loves you even when you're not lovable. God doesn't wait for you to get your act together before He reaches out to you in love. He loves you unconditionally. He calls you to love others the same way. You can do that only out of an overflow of God's love. And you can do it only by an act of the will—by reaching out to the lovable and the unlovable alike.

Love changes people. Sometimes being loved brings out the best in people, makes them more lovable. Sometimes it doesn't. Sometimes people remain selfish or mean or annoying, no matter how much they're loved. But you can be sure of one thing: When you love another person, it changes you. Your attitude toward that person begins to change, and you find it not so hard to love. You can't count on your feelings to lead you to love the people who most need to be loved. But when you commit to obey God's command to love your neighbor and even your enemy, the right feelings follow.

Love
Because God Loves You

What Matters Most...

- God's love for you. God's unconditional love is your motivation to love others.

- Christ's example. He has shown you how to love others by reaching out.

- The Holy Spirit's work. He empowers you to love others.

- Love's transforming power. Love changes you, even when it doesn't change the people you love.

- Your will to obey. Love is a command of God, not a suggestion.

What **Doesn't** Matter...

- The seeming impossibility of loving your enemies. Nothing is impossible with God.

- Your lack of loving feelings. This is about your will, not your feelings.

- The unlovableness of some people. Love them anyway.

- Your own unlovableness. God loves you anyway.

- Other people's ill will even when you're trying to love them. Even then, love them anyway.

Focus Points...

Your great love reaches to the skies, your truth to the clouds.
PSALM 57:10 NCV

Beloved, if God so loved us, we also ought to love one another.
1 JOHN 4:11 NKJV

The steadfast love of the LORD never ceases.
LAMENTATIONS 3:22 NRSV

Know this: GOD, your God, is God indeed, a God you can depend upon. He keeps his covenant of loyal love with those who love him and observe his commandments for a thousand generations.
DEUTERONOMY 7:9 MSG

what really counts

I give you a new commandment: love one another. As I have loved you, so you must love one another.
JOHN 13:34 GNT

Love means to love what is unlovable or it is no love at all.
G. K. CHESTERTON

The single desire that dominated my search for delight was simply to love and to be loved.
SAINT AUGUSTINE

What Matters Most to Me About
Love

Love is a word used to mean a lot of different things. Perhaps the most reliable definition is simply "the act of putting another person's interests ahead of your own." Spend some time reflecting on the role of love in your life.

◎ *Whom do you have a really hard time loving? What can you do to demonstrate the love of Christ?*

_____

_____

_____

_____

_____

_____

_____

◎ *Think about some of the people you love the most. Is your love for them active, reaching out, seeking their best interest? In which ways? Or is your love simply a response to their loveliness?*

_____

_____

_____

_____

_____

_____

_____

what
really
counts

◎ *What is in it for you? How has your life been enriched by loving other people?*

_____
_____
_____
_____
_____
_____
_____
_____
_____
_____

◎ *Think about a time when you were the recipient of love you didn't deserve. How did that make a difference in your life?*

_____
_____
_____
_____
_____
_____
_____
_____
_____
_____

Love is an attribute of God. To love others is evidence of a genuine faith.

KAY ARTHUR

LOVE

GOD'S WORD

An Introduction

> Every word of God is flawless; he is a shield to those who take refuge in him.
>
> PROVERBS 30:5 NIV

Words saturate your world. When you wake up in the morning, you hear the radio announcer making jokes and playing songs. You'll soon catch the news from TV, newspapers, or the Web. Your parents, friends, and teachers add to the nonstop flow of words into your mind. Even people who can't hear are busy communicating with their hands and facial expressions.

As you move throughout your day, you're not just listening; you have plenty of your own words you'd like to share. But words are not all alike. Man-made words are one thing; God-made communication is something entirely different. When you pick up your Bible and read it, something powerful happens. You have a meeting with the Divine Communicator. God's

Word is a "double-edged sword" that cuts deep into your soul and exposes your innermost thoughts.

"Got milk?" "Got God?" "WWJD?" These and others have all become trite marketing expressions. It's easy to think you know what the Bible says without actually reading it on your own. But stepping out into the world without the sword of God's Word means you'll have no offensive weapon to fight evil. You need to be "armed and dangerous," as Ken Abraham wrote.

When you're fueled up on God's wisdom, the apostle John says, "then you will know the truth, and the truth will make you free" (John 8:32 NCV). What a relief! Your life will have purpose and extreme boundaries that nobody can cross. Get ready to rule the world!

Those who walk in truth walk in liberty.
BETH MOORE

God's Word
Sure Thing

Heaven and earth will pass away, but My words will by no means pass away.

MATTHEW 24:35 NKJV

Out with the old, in with the new. Are you caught up in the latest craze for extreme makeovers? There's no denying it—it's fascinating to watch a person or room be completely transformed within a few hours. And designers hope you'll soon be bored with the same old fashions and turn to them for ooh-la-la radical change. If you have the desire and cash, you could be on your way to a whole new look.

Even the Bible has undergone an extreme makeover lately. Teen girls can pick up a copy of the *Revolve* Bible, while guys might like the new look of *Refuel*. The outside covers look more like modern magazines than the stern-looking black leather of the past. A thirteen-year-old girl in Texas joyfully spent her birthday money on this newly made-over Bible, saying it was "fun to read and encouraging."

Though the ultrahip covers might look trendy, the powerful truths inside remain the same. "God's word is alive and working and is sharper than a double-edged sword. It cuts all the way into us, where the soul and the spirit are joined, to the center of our joints and bones. And it judges the thoughts and feelings in our hearts" (Hebrews 4:12 NCV). A new generation is discovering that the Bible's eternal message will never change or go out of style. Author Roger Palms says, "God's Word will not return void . . . It penetrates people's minds; it touches their emotions. They are not the same for having been exposed to God's Word."

Few things in your world will remain the same for centuries. The twin towers of the World Trade Center were reduced to rubble in a matter of minutes. The grassy field you live near today may become a shopping center parking lot in the next decade. Even people you love and trust will come into and go out of your life. But there is one thing you can be sure of: The Bible will never change. Its message will stand true forever. You can read it today, and it will speak to your heart. You can read it in a decade, and the truths will shout at you in your twenties. One day, you'll have God-given wisdom to pass along to your children. Though everything around you may undergo transformation, the Word of God "is eternal; it stands firm in the heavens" (Psalm 119:89 NIV). It's a sure thing.

God's Word
Sure Thing

What Matters Most...

◎ Reading the Bible every day if you can.

◎ Believing it is written by God through the hands of people He chose.

◎ Responding to it. You can't walk away and ignore it.

◎ Opening your heart to a relationship with God through Jesus Christ.

◎ Sharing it with those you care about.

What **Doesn't** Matter...

◎ The outside cover. An extreme outside makeover can't change what's inside.

◎ What your friends think about the Bible. Their opinion is just that.

◎ Knowing as much as your preacher. God speaks to both of you.

◎ Which version you like to read most. What the Bible says is more important than its packaging.

◎ How old you are when you start to read the Bible. Just get started!

Focus Points...

Man shall not live by bread alone; but man lives by every word that proceeds from the mouth of the LORD.
DEUTERONOMY 8:3 NKJV

In the beginning was the one who is called the Word. The Word was with God and was truly God.
JOHN 1:1 CEV

Take these words of mine to heart and keep them in mind. Write them down, tie them around your wrist, and wear them as headbands as a reminder.
DEUTERONOMY 11:18 GOD'S WORD

"Isn't my Message like fire?" GOD's Decree. "Isn't it like a sledgehammer busting a rock?"
JEREMIAH 23:29 MSG

The words of the LORD are pure words, like silver tried in a furnace of earth, purified seven times.
PSALM 12:6 NKJV

The word of God hidden in the heart is a stubborn voice to suppress.

BILLY GRAHAM

Go to the Bible to meet Christ ... He is its author, its subject matter, the doorway to its treasures, the full-throated symphony of which Adam and the prophets heard just the faintest tune.

ANDRE SEU

God's Word

A Light to Your Path

It is written, "Man shall not live by bread alone, but by every word that proceeds from the mouth of God."

MATTHEW 4:4 NKJV

what really counts

When author Elisabeth Elliot was a little girl, she couldn't yet read or write, but she listened to her father read from the big family Bible twice a day. She hid the Scriptures in her heart, not knowing what her future held. The years passed, and as a young college student, she found herself passionately in love with a missionary, Jim Elliot. On her own, she read her Bible every day to remain pure in her feelings for this man. Even though she had no idea where the relationship would lead, she trusted God step by step.

Five years later, Elisabeth married her wonderful dream guy, only to lose him to a sudden, violent death on the mission field in South America. She was thrust into the darkness of being a widow and single mom to her ten-month-old daughter, Valerie. Yet God lit her path, leading her gently through the gut-wrenching despair of loneliness and pain. She wrote, "To me, the commandments, all that the Word of

God comprises, are a lamp . . . He give us enough light for today, enough strength for one day at a time."

Do you ever wish you could see down the path of your life over the next few years to see what God has in store for you? You may wonder what you will do after you graduate. Where will you live? Will you continue school or get married? What kind of work will you be doing? You may sometimes wish God would use a high-powered floodlight to light your way as you stumble into the unknown.

Yet if you could see that far into the future, you might forget your need to spend time in God's Word every day. You may run off into the dark forest alone and get eaten up by a big, bad wolf that you're not prepared to fight. Or you might become so immobilized with fear that you don't attempt anything that requires courage. "Your word like is a lamp for my feet and a light for my path," David wrote in Psalm 119:105 (NCV). You can learn to trust God to show you what you need to get through each day. When you glow with the light of God's Word, you can light the way for others. As Jesus said, "Let your light so shine before men, that they may see your good works and glorify your Father in heaven" (Matthew 5:16 NKJV).

God's Word
A Light to Your Path

What Matters Most...

- Trusting God that He will lead you. He will never mislead you.

- Holding His Word as a lamp that lights your path.

- Waiting on His answer and direction. He will direct your ways.

- Learning from others who are a few steps ahead.

- Living as a light-bearer for the world to see. Let your light shine.

What Doesn't Matter...

- Your fears of the unknown future. God is in control, and He knows what lies ahead.

- Your roller-coaster emotions. Feelings change, but truth doesn't.

- Your past. God loves you and cleanses you through His Word.

- Your youth. God wants to use you NOW to impact your culture.

- Your peers. Focus on what God wants you to believe, not others.

Focus Points...

Break open your words, let the light shine out, let ordinary people see the meaning.
PSALM 119:130 MSG

Be doers of the word, and not merely hearers who deceive themselves.
JAMES 1:22 NRSV

I have always treasured his teachings.
JOB 23:12 CEV

Your word I have treasured in my heart, that I may not sin against You.
PSALM 119:11 NASB

The word is very near you; it is in your mouth and in your heart so you may obey it.
DEUTERONOMY 30:14 NIV

what really counts

God's word is a light not only to our path but to our thinking. Place it in your heart today, and you will never walk in darkness.

JONI EARECKSON TADA

The study of God's word, for the purpose of discovering God's will, is the secret discipline which has formed the greatest characters.

J. W. ALEXANDER

What Matters Most to Me About
God's Word

Knowing God through His Word takes time and energy, just like any other relationship that matters to you. Whenever you read it, God can send you a personal message of guidance, comfort, encouragement, or warning.

◎ *Do you enjoy reading the Bible? Why or why not?*

_____

_____

_____

_____

_____

_____

_____

_____

◎ *God can arrange for you to read a specific passage on the very day you need to hear it. Have you ever felt that God spoke directly to you, using a certain Scripture that you really needed to hear?*

_____

_____

_____

_____

_____

_____

_____

what
really
counts

○ *James compares God's Word to a mirror (see James 1:23–25). In what ways is this true? How does seeing yourself in a real mirror compare to seeing yourself in God's Word?*

_____

_____

_____

_____

_____

_____

_____

_____

○ *Do you have a "life verse," one that you would like to meditate on every day of your life? If not, use this space to write down a verse that is especially meaningful to you.*

_____

_____

_____

_____

_____

_____

_____

_____

The life of faith says, "Lord, You have said it, it appears to be irrational, but I'm going to step out boldly, trusting in Your Word."

OSWALD CHAMBERS

THE FUTURE

An Introduction

> LORD, You are my portion and my cup [of blessing]; You hold my future.
>
> PSALM 16:5 HCSB

what really counts

When you're a student, sometimes it feels as if all you do is prepare for the future. You make the grade so you can get into a good college or graduate program or job. You take a summer internship that pays almost nothing because it will prepare you for a future career. You may even choose your extracurricular activities with an eye to the future, looking to round out a college application or a résumé. You can't help but wonder when you will ever have a chance to live for the present.

The truth is, you will always look to the future. When you finally finish school and get a job, you'll start looking to your future career. If you get married and have kids, you'll be thinking about their future. It's the way human beings are made. Every moment takes you a little further into the future, so you learn to look in that direction. The problem is, even if you're looking that way, you still can't truly see anything. You can predict, you can guess, you can hope, but you can't see.

But there is Someone who can see the future. For God, all time is in the present tense—past, present, and future. There's no way for time-bound human beings to get their minds around such a thing. But you can take comfort and confidence from the fact that the God who directs your steps is already in your future, and He already has it prepared for your arrival.

It is never safe to look into the future with eyes of fear.
E. H. HARRIMAN

The Future
The God Who Holds the Future

Live carefree before God; he is
most careful with you.

1 PETER 5:7 MSG

Do you ever feel that the future is barreling down on you
like a runaway freight train? Graduation is coming, everybody wants to know what your future plans are, and you
don't have any idea what to tell them. Or maybe you have the
opposite problem. Maybe it feels like the future is never going
to get here. Your life feels like one big holding pattern, and
you can't seem to get cleared for landing. Either way, you're
experiencing one of those built-in dilemmas that all human
beings experience. God gave you the ability to think about the
future, but He didn't give you the ability to control it.

The good news, however, is that the future is in better
hands than yours. You may not know what the future holds,
but you do know what kind of God holds the future. You
know that God is all-loving. Like anyone else who truly loves
you, He wants what's best for you. He rejoices to see His people prosper. Sometimes people who want what's best for you

114

don't actually know what's best for you, or they may be unable to make it happen. But with God, that's not the case. God is all-knowing; down to the smallest detail, He knows what's best for all His creatures. He is also all-powerful; no power in the universe can stop Him from carrying out His plan.

"'I know the plans I have for you,' says the LORD. 'They are plans for good and not for disaster, to give you a future and a hope'" (Jeremiah 29:11 NLT). You have a future and a hope. More than that, you have a future that is defined by hope. Hope is a lot more than a vague wish. It's a confidence that you are moving into a future that a good God holds in His hands. Hope is the belief that you don't have to know all the details of what lies ahead, because you are confident that all things ultimately work for your benefit and everlasting happiness.

Your future is bright. It's bright beyond belief. That's not to say your future won't hold some difficult times. But you can be sure in the difficult times, no less than in the good times, that the God of the universe has a plan to do you good. And His plans cannot be thwarted.

The Future
The God Who Holds the Future

What Matters Most...

- ◉ God's faithfulness. He never changes.

- ◉ God's love. He wants what's best for you even when you don't.

- ◉ God's omniscience. He knows what's best for you.

- ◉ God's omnipotence. He cannot be prevented from doing what's best for you.

- ◉ God's omnipresence. He is with you all the time.

What Doesn't Matter...

- ◉ Doubt. Even when you doubt, God is faithful.

- ◉ Fears. Everything is in God's hands, and you can trust your life to his.

- ◉ The past. That's not what ultimately determines the future.

- ◉ Time wasted. It's not too late to get with God's program for your life.

- ◉ Second-guessing. God knows what He's doing even when you don't know what's ahead.

Focus Points...

Do not worry about tomorrow, for tomorrow will worry about its own things. Sufficient for the day is its own trouble.
MATTHEW 6:34 NKJV

Don't fret or worry. Instead of worrying, pray. Let petitions and praises shape your worries into prayers, letting God know your concerns.
PHILIPPIANS 4:6 MSG

You, LORD God, have done many wonderful things, and you have planned marvelous things for us. No one is like you! I would never be able to tell all you have done.
PSALM 40:5 CEV

Keep your eye on the healthy soul, scrutinize the straight life; there's a future in strenuous wholeness.
PSALM 37:37 MSG

what really counts

God will not allow man to have a knowledge of things to come; for if he had prescience of his prosperity, he would be careless; and if understanding of his adversity, he would be despairing and senseless.

SAINT AUGUSTINE

Prediction is very difficult, especially about the future.
NEILS BOHR

The Future
New Heaven, New Earth

> I saw a new heaven and a new earth.
> REVELATION 21:1 CEV

The law of entropy, roughly paraphrased, states that everything in the universe tends to disintegrate toward chaos. You see the law of entropy at work in your bedroom. If you're not cleaning it on a regular basis, it quickly slides toward chaos. You see it when a young, inexperienced substitute gets assigned to a class of grade-school rowdies. It doesn't take long before any sense of order imposed by the regular teacher dissolves into total chaos. You see it in your personal relationships; people naturally grow apart if they're not working hard to stay together.

The law of entropy would suggest that the future is one of more disorder, more suffering, more chaos until the universe finally grinds to a halt. But the law of entropy doesn't account for the intervention of God, who promises to repair the disintegration that has afflicted His creation and create a new heaven and a new earth. All the sadness, all the sickness, all the ruin of this messy life will feel like a distant dream: "God himself will be with them and will be their God. He will wipe away every tear from their eyes, and there will be no more death, sadness, crying, or pain, because all the old ways are gone" (Revelation 21:3–4 NCV). That's the kind of future you have to look forward to.

Sometimes life is so messy and chaotic that you lose hope it will ever feel normal again. Sometimes you drift so far that you don't think you could ever get back on track. But that's not true. Chaos is just raw material for God the Creator, God the Sustainer. He can reach into a life and shape its wreckage into something good. He delights to speak grace into a messy life and bring hope where before there was no hope.

Apart from God's promise, all you can expect is a slow slide into chaos. It's the law of a sin-cursed universe: Entropy gets everybody in the end. Bodies disintegrate, relationships fall apart, and cars break down. But that's not cause for despair. It's cause to turn to the God who promised to make all things new. The creation is groaning under the weight of its servitude to corruption and decay. You, too, experience it every time you suffer loss or disappointment. But one day there will be a new heaven and a new earth. All creation—including you—has a future and a hope.

The Future
New Heaven, New Earth

What Matters Most...

◉ Living God's promise. You have nothing to stress about; you can rest on God's promise.

◉ Pressing on. You have a future to look forward to, and God is leading you to it.

◉ Sharing hope. You have good news to tell.

◉ Thanking God. He's doing great things for you, and every day He does more.

◉ Singing God's praises. It's good practice for the new heaven and new earth.

What Doesn't Matter...

◉ The law of entropy. God is doing a new thing.

◉ The seeming inevitability of disintegration. God over-rules.

◉ Uncertainty. It's not up to you to know all the details, nor is it even possible.

◉ Your lack of control over the future. God has it well in hand.

◉ Worry. You can rest in God's faithfulness.

Focus Points...

All creation is eagerly waiting for God to show who his children are. Meanwhile, creation is confused, but not because it wants to be confused. God made it this way in the hope that creation would be set free from decay and would share in the glorious freedom of his children.
ROMANS 8:19–21 CEV

He is before all things, and in Him all things hold together.
COLOSSIANS 1:17 NASB

He'll banish death forever. And GOD will wipe the tears from every face. He'll remove every sign of disgrace from his people, wherever they are. Yes! GOD says so!
ISAIAH 25:8 MSG

what really counts

This body that can be destroyed must clothe itself with something that can never be destroyed. And this body that dies must clothe itself with something that can never die.
1 CORINTHIANS 15:53 NCV

Heaven wheels above you, displaying to you her eternal glories, and still your eyes are on the ground.
DANTE ALIGHIERI

Hope is not the conviction that something will turn out well, but the certainty that something makes sense regardless of how it turns out.
BARBARA JOHNSON

121

What Matters Most to Me About
The Future

The future is coming. Are you ready to deal with it? Take some time to write down your thoughts about the future that awaits you.

◎ *What are your hopes for the future? Who do you want to be in future years? Turn those hopes into a written prayer.*

_____

_____

_____

_____

what
really
counts

_____

_____

_____

◎ *What about your fears for the future? Turn those into a prayer as well.*

_____

_____

_____

_____

_____

_____

_____

Life is lived looking forward, but only understood looking back. Look back on a time when you were looking forward to now. How would your hopes and fears have been different if you had known then what you know now?

_____

_____

_____

_____

_____

_____

_____

_____

_____

Is concern for the future keeping you from living in the present? Write some ways that God's all-knowing, all-powerful, all-loving character makes it possible for you to let go and live today.

_____

_____

_____

_____

_____

_____

_____

_____

_____

Trust the past to God's mercy, the present to
God's love and the future to God's providence.
SAINT AUGUSTINE

WORSHIP

An Introduction

Bow down and worship the LORD our Creator!
PSALM 95:6 CEV

what really counts

There's nothing quite like the feeling you get when you wake up and realize it's your birthday. The sun seems a little brighter, the air smells a little fresher, and you can't wait to see who's going to greet you with that cheerful birthday wish. When you were a kid, your parents might have gone a little overboard and thrown you a theme party that focused on your favorite hobby or cartoon character. All day long, every card, e-mail, and lick of icing made you feel like you were on top of the world, simply because you were born.

In contrast, it would be a real downer if nobody remembered it was your birthday and you went around feeling like you'd been forgotten. Yet how often do God's people forget to worship Him and celebrate His glory? Every single breath you take is a gift from God; He created you and loves you as His child. But do you ever get so busy or caught up in your own world that you forget to even acknowledge Him?

When you step outside yourself for a minute and focus on who God is, He fills that void in your heart that nothing else will fill. Author Sam Storms said, "Worship is a feast in which God is the host, the cook, the waiter, and the meal itself." When you take the time to celebrate God through praise and worship, He turns around and blesses you with the rich fullness of joy.

> If worship does not propel us into greater obedience, it has not been worship. To stand before the Holy One of eternity is to change.
>
> RICHARD FOSTER

Worship
Stepping Outside Yourself

> God is Spirit, and those who worship Him must worship in spirit and truth.
>
> JOHN 4:24 NKJV

what really counts

Being a student is sometimes like being up on a stage, in the bright heat of a spotlight. It's all about you: your dreams, your goals, your future. You look around and compare yourself to your friends to see how you're doing. Sometimes you're way ahead of the pack, and you feel a little smug—you got the better grade, the cooler summer job, or the bigger scholarship. Other times you bomb, like an embarrassing act in a talent show. But always, always, you feel as though every eye is upon you, watching each move you make.

The truth is, you're not the one in the spotlight; God is. If you constantly live each day thinking that you are the center of the universe, you will miss out on the true center of your life. Everyone thought Copernicus was a complete moron when he dared to propose that the earth revolved around the sun instead of vice versa. Nobody is laughing at him now.

Our lives revolve around God. The only way to step out

of our self-contained worlds is to "set our eyes not on what we see but on what we cannot see. What we see will last only a short time, but what we cannot see will last forever" (2 Corinthians 4:18 NCV). You can't see God, but when you worship Him, He transforms you into the kind of person He wants you to be. The Hebrew word for worship is *shachah,* which means "to prostrate oneself, bow down, fall down flat, do reverence." This is how you would have responded in the presence of an earthly king, and this is how you should respond to being in the presence of the almighty Ruler of all creation.

Songwriter and worship leader Matt Redman said, "Worship is about getting personal with God, drawing close to God." This can take place anywhere you decide to lift your thoughts heavenward instead of inward. You can praise God when you observe His beauty in nature, such as in the rise of the full moon or in the splendor of a golden fall leaf. You can worship God when you sing spiritually uplifting songs in your car or on your way to class. When you can step beyond your own problems and focus on who is behind it all, you realize the truth in Pastor Rick Warren's statement: "It's not about you."

Worship
Stepping Outside Yourself

What Matters Most...

- Stepping outside yourself to enter the presence of God. He's there, waiting for you, expecting you.

- Treating your relationship with God as your first priority in life.

- Realizing how small your problems are compared to how great God is.

- Making worship a daily habit. It can take place anywhere: in church, outside, or in your car.

- Responding to God's desire to transform you. Don't walk away without desiring to obey.

What Doesn't Matter...

- Putting yourself in the spotlight. It's not about you.

- Having a mushy, feel-good experience. Worship can be a frame of mind.

- Being able to sing well. Your voice is interceded by the Holy Spirit and sounds awesome to God.

- Comparing your worship life to others'. People express themselves in different ways.

- Feeling like you are too young to know God in a dynamic, personal way. Your youth can be an encouragement to older, worn-out believers.

Focus Points...

I bless you every time I take a breath; my arms wave like banners of praise to you.

PSALM 63:4 MSG

You shall obey me, the LORD, who brought you out of Egypt with great power and strength; you are to bow down to me and offer sacrifices to me.

2 KINGS 17:36 GNT

Worship the Lord your God, and serve him only.

MATTHEW 4:10 NIV

He is wonderful! Praise him and bring an offering into his temple. Worship the LORD, majestic and holy.

1 CHRONICLES 16:29 CEV

Serve the LORD with gladness; come before His presence with singing.

PSALM 100:2 NKJV

what really counts

Through worship, a right ordering of God, the world, self, and neighbor is experienced, and the worshiper receives a peace that passes understanding. Simply put, worship is an it-is-well-with-my-soul experience.

ROBERT WEBBER

If God were small enough to be understood, He would not be big enough to be worshiped.

EVELYN UNDERHILL

129

Worship
Fullness of Joy

> Everything on earth will worship you;
> they will sing your praises, shouting
> your name in glorious songs.
>
> PSALM 66:4 NLT

Have you ever cruised home on an empty tank of gas, holding your breath and hoping you'd be able to make it to the station the next day? It's not a load of fun. What if you were to get in your car the next morning and see a sticky note attached to your steering wheel from your dear old dad: "Hope you don't mind—I thought you could use some gas, so I filled her up." You'd feel like thanking him right away, no doubt. It's the same way with God—He wants you to acknowledge all the good things He has done for you as well.

This is what worship is all about: responding to God's powerful gift of love. When you first become a Christian, it is an amazing act simply to accept the free gift of salvation that's been given you. Receiving is your first step of faith. But as you grow spiritually, you'll feel empty if all you do is keep taking and not give anything back in return. You'll wonder why you're not happy and not growing. It's because you're missing out on the joy of worship.

David said it best when he wrote, "You have made known to me the path of life; you will fill me with joy in your presence" (Psalm 16:11 NIV). There were so many times in David's life when he had no earthly reason to be joyful: His brothers made fun of him, he had a boring job, and then King Saul got insanely jealous of him and wanted to kill him. In time, he lost his best friend, spent months hiding out in dark caves, and watched his child grow sick and die. Where did he turn? To the presence of God, where he found forgiveness, peace, and joy.

Nothing that happens to you in life is going to give you that deep, rich fullness of joy unless you learn to continually give thanks to God. Yet when you feel empty inside, you may try to fill up on things that don't satisfy, such as money, love, and power. Songwriter Graham Kendrick wrote, "Everybody worships. Whether it is a hero, possessions, success, pleasure, a political cause, a carved idol or oneself, the way we live and behave makes evident the things we love and give ourselves to." As David learned, it takes a step of faith to learn to worship the Giver instead of His gifts.

Worship
Fullness of Joy

What Matters Most...

- Realizing your innate need to worship. You were designed to praise your Creator.

- Praising God with your whole heart and not just your lips. *Really* get into worship!

- Thanking God for all His good gifts. He's given you your life, your family, and your friends.

- Developing an attitude of humility before God. A thankful heart is a humble heart.

- Loving God above all else in your life. He's the true source of everything good.

What **Doesn't** Matter...

- Knowledge. If you feel like you don't know the right words to say, just read a few psalms aloud.

- Happiness. It comes or goes based on your circumstances. Seek the joy of the Lord instead.

- Insecurities. Don't worry what others think as you give yourself freedom to worship.

- Past failures. God is always ready for you to take a new step toward Him.

- Worldly success or failure. God sees you as perfect in His sight and wants to use you based on your faith.

Focus Points...

I proclaim the name of the LORD: Ascribe greatness to our God.
DEUTERONOMY 32:3 NKJV

Don't worship any other god, because I, the LORD, the Jealous One, am a jealous God.
EXODUS 34:14 NCV

Worship the LORD in holy attire; tremble before Him, all the earth.
PSALM 96:9 NASB

I beseech you therefore, brethren, by the mercies of God, that you present your bodies a living sacrifice, holy, acceptable to God, which is your reasonable service.
ROMANS 12:1 NKJV

what
really
counts

Sing to GOD a brand-new song, sing his praises all over the world! Let the sea and its fish give a round of applause, with all the far-flung islands joining in.
ISAIAH 42:10 MSG

Whenever you get a blessing from God, give it back to him as a love gift. Take time to meditate before God and offer the blessing back to him in a deliberate act of worship.
OSWALD CHAMBERS

When I worship, I would rather my heart be without words than my words be without heart.
LAMAR BOSCHMAN

What Matters Most to Me About
Worship

Worship is all about celebrating the presence of God in your life. It's a chance for you to focus on your heavenly Father instead of on yourself. Take a few minutes to reflect on your worship experiences.

◎ *Some worship services celebrate the birth, death, and resurrection of Christ. What are some ways the church prepares for these special services? How can you best prepare your heart for worship?*

_____

_____

_____

_____

_____

_____

_____

◎ *Is there a certain time or place where you feel really close to God? Why?*

_____

_____

_____

_____

_____

_____

what
really
counts

◎ *Do you have a favorite song or Scripture that you enjoy using when you worship God?*

_____

_____

_____

_____

_____

_____

_____

_____

◎ *What are some things that hold you back when you think about worshiping God? How can you overcome these hindrances?*

_____

_____

_____

_____

_____

_____

_____

_____

_____

> Worship is a voluntary act of gratitude offered by the saved to the Savior, by the healed to the Healer, and by the delivered to the Deliverer.
>
> MAX LUCADO

THE CHURCH

An Introduction

> Where two or three are gathered together in My name, I am there in the midst of them.
>
> MATTHEW 18:20 NKJV

what really counts

If you've ever been camping before, you know one of the first things you do is build a good campfire. You don't just look around and find one great log; instead, you pick out at least half a dozen smaller ones, and some kindling as well. Then you can light a fire that will burn for hours, allowing you to drink that steaming cup of hot chocolate along with your roasted hot dogs and s'mores.

In the same way that one log won't sustain a decent campfire, your Christian faith will fizzle out if you try to keep the flame going on your own. Martin Luther said, "At home, in my house, there is no warmth or vigor in me, but in the church when the multitude is gathered together, a fire is kindled in my heart and it breaks its way through." The purpose of meeting together for fellowship is to glorify God through worship, grow in your faith through instruction from godly teachers, and serve others in the community using your talents and gifts.

You have an important place in God's family. The church is designed with Christ at the head, and each member makes up various parts of the body. By finding out what your spiritual gifts are, you'll know right where you can plug in and fan that flame of Christian fellowship. As Gigi Graham Tchividjian said, "We are not equally blessed with great intellect or physical beauty or emotional strength. But we have all been given the same ability to be faithful."

There are many things which a person can do alone, but being a Christian is not one of them . . . The personal relationship to Christ can only be realized when one has "come to himself" as a member of His Body, the Christian fellowship.

WILLIAM T. HAM

The Church
Ordinary People, Extraordinary Purpose

We are his house, built on the foundation
of the apostles and the prophets. And the
cornerstone is Christ Jesus himself
EPHESIANS 2:20 NLT

Take a stroll through Hebrews 11 sometime, and you'll feel as if you're in a museum lined with portraits of the great spiritual heroes of the Bible. The chapter that is often referred to as the Hall of Faith is like a receiving line of God's chosen ones. You'll see Noah there, and Abraham, along with his sons, Isaac and Jacob. Then Joseph shows up, Moses, David, and many more prophets. But what's surprising about these quick portraits is not how grand and majestic their lives were, but how deep the people's faith was.

In every example in this chapter, God used ordinary people to accomplish a noble purpose because of their complete trust in Him. And God wants to use you, too. Do you sometimes feel that you don't have all that much to offer God? You're laying the foundation now for your whole life, and there's no better time than now to prepare. When you're a student, you can learn to discern God's voice from voices in the crowd and dream big for Him. You've heard the saying "Aim for nothing, and you'll hit it every time." But if you make it your goal to aim for God Himself, you can't miss.

The very fact that you're reading a book like this one shows that God's already got His hand on your life. Whether you bought it yourself or received it as a gift, you're learning that the things that matter most to God are the things that should matter most to you. When Jesus went around choosing His twelve disciples, He didn't go to the prominent cities gathering respected scholars and leaders; instead, He went to the seaport and found some humble fishermen who had teachable hearts and attitudes. He didn't gather around those who were perfect, with no stain of sin in their pasts; He chose tax collectors, prostitutes, and people who were diseased and demon-possessed to be set free from their pain and proclaim His message to their family and friends.

It's God's choice to fill up His church with all types of people. He has a special place in His heart for those who have teachable hearts and deep faith. When God's people gather together and combine their many talents and gifts, amazing things can happen. Battles can be won, kingdoms can be gained, and souls can be led to salvation. Your journey of a thousand miles begins with only a tiny step of faith.

The Church
Ordinary People, Extraordinary Purpose

What Matters Most...

- Passion for God. Let God ignite the fire in your heart that will give your life purpose.

- Deep faith and trust. God has a perfect plan for you.

- An attitude of humility. Don't block out His voice with your pride.

- A teachable heart. Desire to please God above all else.

- Obedience. It all starts with a small step, but it leads to the way everlasting.

What Doesn't Matter...

- Outside appearance. God sees you as unique and perfect in His eyes.

- Education level. Let your heart be filled with biblical wisdom, not the world's view of knowledge.

- Experience. The only way you gain experience is to take risks, fail, and try again.

- Status in society. God uses the humble to shame the proud.

- Wealth. Let your treasure be in things that are eternal, not temporary.

Focus Points...

Since we are surrounded by such a great cloud of witnesses, let us ... run with perseverance the race marked out for us.
HEBREWS 12:1 NIV

Let us consider how we may spur one another on toward love and good deeds.
HEBREWS 10:24 NIV

Just as iron sharpens iron, friends sharpen the minds of each other.
PROVERBS 27:17 CEV

You Gentiles are ... citizens along with all of God's holy people. You are members of God's family.
EPHESIANS 2:19 NLT

what really counts

In him you too are being built together to become a dwelling in which God lives by his Spirit.
EPHESIANS 2:22 NIV

Every Christian community must realize that not only do the weak need the strong, but also that the strong cannot exist without the weak. The elimination of the weak is the death of the fellowship.

DIETRICH BONHOEFFER

It does not take a perfect church to introduce a man to the perfect Christ.

RICHARD WOODSOME

The Church
The Body

> We, who are many, are one body in Christ, and individually members one of another.
>
> ROMANS 12:5 NASB

what really counts

When you're sitting in a padded church pew on a typical Sunday morning, it may be tempting to forget that there are people around the globe spilling their blood every day to have that freedom. Try to make it one of your goals to visit a worship service in at least one other country during your lifetime. It's best to go when you're a student, before you get tied down and committed to responsibilities that would prevent you from traveling abroad. You'll never be the same.

All over the planet, the Christian Church is one church, one body. When you sing in English on Sunday mornings, there are thousands of people singing the very same melodies in Chinese, Russian, Swahili, and other languages. They are holding their Bibles and reading the same Scriptures in different language translations. Each person in God's family has been chosen by Him and has something to offer the body of Christ as a whole.

Have you thought about what you can offer the body of Christ? One of the best ways you can serve God now while you are a student is to find out how you can plug into serving others in your church. Do you like kids? There is nothing a tired mom appreciates more than an energetic nursery worker who can entertain her wiggly toddler while she attends the worship service. Are you good at sports? See if you can help arrange outdoor games for kids at Bible school, retreats, and camps. Use your athletic abilities to teach and inspire your church family to take care of their own health.

Are you good at organizing? See if you can volunteer in the church office, classrooms, or library arranging books and supplies. Short on time? You can always make a few phone calls. "We missed you last Sunday" and "Is there anything you'd like me to pray about for you?" are phrases that can go a long way toward reaching out to people.

In the same way that each organ in the human body plays an important role in life, you're an integral part of the global church body. Right now, you may feel like an elbow or a pinkie finger instead of a vital organ like a lung or a kidney. But when combined with the fellowship of other parts of the body of Christ, you form a whole church that's going to make an impact for the kingdom of God.

The Church
The Body

What Matters Most...

◎ Your spiritual gifts. Find out what they are and learn to plug in to your church and community.

◎ The global Christian family. Everyone serves the same God, worshiping Him in different ways, in different languages.

◎ Fellowship with other believers. Roles are combined in the body of Christ to make the body alive.

◎ Your willingness to serve others. It may be something as simple as a phone call, but it does make a difference.

◎ Your focus as a church. Keep your eyes on glorifying God.

What Doesn't Matter...

◎ Your fears. Don't be afraid to step out in a leadership role using your spiritual gifts.

◎ Your past. God renews your mind every day, and you should dwell on the future, not the past.

◎ Your feelings. They're not as important as your faith. Even Moses was scared that he stuttered, and yet look what he accomplished!

◎ Your age. Now's the time to get going and join a service corps while you have your whole life ahead of you.

◎ Your limited time. Each minute counts. Time can be wasted, or it can be spent learning and doing something useful for God.

Focus Points...

Even as the body is one and yet has many members, and all the members of the body, though they are many, are one body, so also is Christ.
1 CORINTHIANS 12:12 NASB

Exhort one another daily, while it is called "Today," lest any of you be hardened through the deceitfulness of sin.
HEBREWS 3:13 NKJV

You should not stay away from the church meetings, as some are doing, but you should meet together and encourage each other. Do this even more as you see the day coming.
HEBREWS 10:25 NCV

You are Peter, and I can guarantee that on this rock I will build my church. And the gates of hell will not overpower it.
MATTHEW 16:18 GOD'S WORD

what really counts

I go to church, not because of any legalistic or moralistic reasons, but because I am a hungry sheep who needs to be fed; and for the same reason that I wear a wedding ring: a public witness of a private commitment.

MADELEINE L'ENGLE

Aloneness can lead to loneliness . . . In Christ we have the capacity for the fulfilling sense of belonging which comes from intimate fellowship with God and with other believers.

NEIL T. ANDERSON

What Matters Most to Me About
The Church

When you enter the family of God through your faith in Jesus, you become part of the body of Christ. He is the Head, and you are part of the body that will build Him up and bring Him glory. Take a few minutes to think about your role in the church.

◎ *Have you ever taken a survey of your spiritual gifts? Talk to someone in your church or find a book that contains a test. What do you think your gifts are?*

_____

_____

_____

_____

_____

_____

_____

_____

◎ *How do you think God can use you in the church to bring Him glory and to serve others?*

_____

_____

_____

_____

_____

_____

_____

_____

what
really
counts

◎ *Do you think you have the kind of faith that will take you from being ordinary to extraordinary? What helps or hinders you in your faith?*

_____

_____

_____

_____

_____

_____

_____

_____

_____

◎ *Write down one of your favorite fellowship experiences that has taken place within God's family.*

_____

_____

_____

_____

_____

_____

_____

_____

_____

Christians are like flowers in a garden: they have upon them the dew of heaven, which, being shaken by the wind, they let fall at each other's roots, whereby they are jointly nourished.

JOHN BUNYAN

WISDOM

An Introduction

> Happy is the person who finds wisdom, the one who gets understanding. Wisdom is worth more than silver; it brings more profit than gold.
>
> PROVERBS 3:13–14 NCV

what really counts

You might define wisdom as knowing what really counts—and not just knowing, but making everyday decisions based on that knowledge. Wisdom means valuing that which is truly valuable and letting go of everything else. Jesus told a parable about a man who found a magnificent pearl buried in a field. He sold everything he had to buy the field. That's wisdom in a nutshell: selling things of lesser value so that you can buy up the things that are truly valuable.

Here's another way of saying the same thing: Wisdom is knowing what's really going to make you happy—eternally happy—and going after those things instead of fleeting pleasures. The book of Proverbs is a compendium of wisdom. In its many observations, an outline for skillful living begins to emerge. "The eyes of a fool are on the ends of the earth" (Proverbs 17:24 NASB), but a wise person knows that real joy is closer to home. Real joy is putting together a life of substance, a life lived for a higher purpose than pleasure or popularity or good grades.

What are you spending your life on? Are you trading your valuable time for things that are even more valuable, or are you throwing it away on things that are cheap and short-lived? Pursue what really counts. Buy wisdom. Search for it "like a prospector panning for gold, like an adventurer on a treasure hunt" (Proverbs 2:4 MSG). You'll never make a better investment.

> The art of being wise is the art of knowing what to overlook.
>
> WILLIAM JAMES

Wisdom
The Power of Imagination

The revelation of GOD is whole and pulls our lives together. The signposts of GOD are clear and point out the right road.

PSALM 19:7 MSG

It had been a long day of hunting. Esau was tired and hungry. He was still a good distance from the family camp when he first smelled the stew that his brother Jacob was cooking. The closer he got, the better it smelled. And the better it smelled, the hungrier he got. By the time he reached the cooking fire, he was fainting with hunger. He had to have a bowl of that stew. "Please," he said to his brother, "feed me some stew, for I am weary." Jacob wasn't nearly as brawny and outdoorsy as his brother, Esau. But he was shrewd. He didn't dish up the stew immediately. "I'll give you some stew," he answered. "But only on one condition: sell me your birthright." Esau was the elder brother even though they were twins, and by rights he would be the head of the family and the owner of all the family property when their father, Isaac, died.

150

Esau looked around him. The family property was just a big desert. Some birthright. Sure, God had promised their grandfather Abraham that his family would become a great nation. But here they were at the third generation, and the "great nation" consisted of two brothers who didn't get along very well. Under the circumstances, the birthright seemed a mighty vague notion. But that bowl of stew—there was nothing vague about that. It was right there in front of him. He could see it; he could smell it. And if he gave up his so-called birthright, he could also taste it. So he did. "What good is a birthright to me if I starve to death?" he asked. He sold away his inheritance—the entire nation of Israel—for a bowl of stew.

Wisdom is about imagination. Esau's unwise decision was basically a failure of imagination. He lacked the imagination to picture what God had promised: his family as a great nation living in a land flowing with milk and honey. He saw a dusty landscape and a not-too-promising family. And he saw a bowl of stew.

What about you? Do you have the imagination to value the not-yet promises of God over the right-here pleasures and amusements that surround you? Can you pass up a bowl of stew if it means selling your stake in God's promises? That kind of imagination is a good start toward real wisdom.

Wisdom
The Power of Imagination

What Matters Most...

- Believing God. Wisdom requires faith.

- Valuing things rightly. Wise people know and embrace what matters.

- Foresight. Wise people can picture the consequences of their actions.

- Insight. Wise people don't just know; they understand.

- Hindsight. Wise people heed and learn from lessons of the past.

What Doesn't Matter...

- Short-term gains—if they cost you long-term rewards.

- Anything that prevents you from laying hold of your birthright. Don't sell it too cheaply.

- Inability to predict the future. See with eyes of faith.

- Lack of wisdom. Pray for God's wisdom, and He will give it to you.

- Doubts. God keeps His promises, so you need never worry.

Focus Points...

Respect and obey the LORD! This is the first step to wisdom and good sense. God will always be respected.
PSALM 111:10 CEV

Happy is the person who finds wisdom, the one who gets understanding.
PROVERBS 3:13 NCV

It is senseless to pay tuition to educate a fool who has no heart for wisdom.
PROVERBS 17:16 NLT

Real wisdom, God's wisdom, begins with a holy life and is characterized by getting along with others. It is gentle and reasonable, overflowing with mercy and blessings, not hot one day and cold the next, not two-faced.
JAMES 3:17 MSG

what really counts

Wisdom is the power to see and the inclination to choose the best and highest goal, together with the surest means of attaining it.

J. I. PACKER

Wisdom is knowledge applied. Head knowledge is useless on the battlefield. Knowledge stamped on the heart makes one wise.

BETH MOORE

153

Wisdom
You Want It, You Got It

> We speak the wisdom of God in a mystery, the hidden wisdom which God ordained before the ages for our glory.
>
> 1 CORINTHIANS 2:7 NKJV

A child sits across from her mother, and on the table between them are a bowl of chocolate kisses, a plate of cookies, and a bowl of broccoli. The child eyes her choices, then says, "May I have the broccoli?" How do you think the mother would respond? "Of course you can have the broccoli! As much as you want. Have some candy and a couple of cookies, too!" What parent wouldn't be thrilled to fill a child's request when the child asks for what's best for her and the parent has ample store of the thing requested?

God promises to give wisdom to anyone who asks for it. "If any of you lacks wisdom, let him ask of God, who gives to all liberally and without reproach, and it will be given to him" (James 1:5 NKJV). And why wouldn't He give generously? He wants nothing more for His children than for them to be wise, and He has no shortage of wisdom to give them. You may remember the story of King Solomon. God offered to give him anything he asked for, and Solomon asked for wisdom to rule the Israelites. God was so pleased that Solomon asked for wisdom instead of riches or power, He gave him not only the wisdom he asked for, but also the money and power he didn't ask for (see 1 Kings 3).

Wisdom is often associated with older people. And there's a certain truth in that. Older people have made more mistakes than you have, and have so earned an extra measure of wisdom. Life experience often teaches people about what makes other people tick and how the world goes around. But many years' hard experience isn't the only path for acquiring wisdom. You can also get it by asking for it. That doesn't mean God will just pump wisdom directly into your head and heart. You gain wisdom by marinating yourself in Scripture and prayer, and trusting God to apply that wisdom to your life—to transform it from head knowledge to a changed way of living.

Wisdom, when you boil it down, is about wanting the same things God wants for you—wanting them enough to do them, or to get them. Just by the act of wanting wisdom, you're paving the way toward wisdom. More than that, when you want wisdom, on some level you have already become wise.

Wisdom
You Want It, You Got It

What Matters Most...

◎ Making the request. Wisdom is yours for the asking.

◎ Seeking. God doesn't zap you with wisdom. He applies it to you as you seek it in His Word.

◎ Your desire. How much do you want to be wise? Read Scripture, study, and pray.

◎ God's supply. He has no shortage of wisdom to give, and He will give it generously.

◎ God's generosity. He loves to give good gifts, and He often gives more than you ask.

What **Doesn't** Matter...

◎ Youth. You aren't too young to be wise.

◎ Lack of experience. Experience isn't the only teacher.

◎ Position. You don't have to hold an important position to be wise.

◎ Mistakes. God uses those, too, to grow you in wisdom.

◎ Lack of influence. It's better to have wisdom without influence than influence without wisdom.

Focus Points...

Give to Your servant an understanding heart to judge Your people, that I [Solomon] may discern between good and evil.

1 Kings 3:9 NKJV

Do not be wise in your own eyes; fear the Lord and depart from evil.

Proverbs 3:7 NKJV

It's written, I'll turn conventional wisdom on its head, I'll expose so-called experts as crackpots.

1 Corinthians 1:19 MSG

Let us, then, feel very sure that we can come before God's throne where there is grace. There we can receive mercy and grace to help us when we need it.

Hebrews 4:16 NCV

what really counts

As we trust God to give us wisdom for today's decisions, He will lead us a step at a time into what He wants us to be doing in the future.

Theodore Epp

God guides us first through his Word, then through our heartfelt desires, then the wise counsel of others, and then our circumstances. At that point we must rely on our own sound judgment . . . God gave each of us a brain, and he expects us to put it to good use.

Bruce K. Waltke

What Matters Most to Me About
Wisdom

Wisdom is yours for the asking. But it doesn't come all at once; nor does it come without some effort on your part. Spend some time reflecting on the importance of wisdom in your life.

◎ *Wisdom is about shaping your everyday life around what is truly valuable. If someone were to follow you around and observe your every action for a week, what would he or she say you value?*

_____

_____

_____

_____

what
really
counts

_____

_____

◎ *What mistakes have you made that have added to your store of wisdom? How about the mistakes of others?*

_____

_____

_____

_____

_____

_____

_____

You face decisions that will require lots of wisdom. Write a prayer asking God for the wisdom you need.

_____

_____

_____

_____

_____

_____

_____

_____

_____

Think of a person whose wisdom you admire. How is that person different from other people you know?

_____

_____

_____

_____

_____

_____

_____

_____

_____

Wisdom is the reward you get for a lifetime of listening when you would have preferred to talk.
DOUG LARSON

WISDOM

PURPOSE

An Introduction

> Behold, God is mighty, but despises no one; He is mighty in strength of understanding.
>
> JOB 36:5 NKJV

what really counts

It's amazing how everything God created in nature has order and purpose. He made some animals extra colorful to scare away their enemies. He gave flowers their stunning beauty to attract insects and birds that help with pollination. Every animal is born with features and habits that enable it to survive. Humans are no different. God made each part of your body with definite tasks to accomplish, and He created each human soul for a special purpose. That means God made you for an incredible reason.

Many people spend their whole lives searching for God's will and purpose. The book of Ecclesiastes describes one such search. The wisest man who ever lived, King Solomon, was on a passionate quest for the meaning of life. He was a guy who had it all: a fabulous palace full of luxuries, power to do anything he wanted, and admiration of society and of God. He searched for life's meaning in the pleasures of eating, drinking, and being merry; none of that was fulfilling. Nor did he find that man's purpose was just to work hard at a given job. In the end, Solomon concluded, "Everything has been heard, so I give my final advice: Honor God and obey his commands, because this is all people must do" (Ecclesiastes 12:13 NCV). Honor God. Obey His commands. The wisest man in the world spent a lifetime figuring that out. It seems simple, but if you're serious about understanding what it means in your life, it might take a lifetime.

> Knowing that we are fulfilling God's purpose is the only thing that really gives rest to the restless human heart.
>
> CHARLES COLSON

Purpose
What's Your Major?

God is working in you, giving you the desire to obey him and the power to do what pleases him.
PHILIPPIANS 2:13 NLT

what really counts

When you're getting close to your senior year in high school, people love asking you the question "What do you want to major in?" Likewise, every time a college student meets someone new, he is bombarded with "So what's your major?" It's easy to fall into the trap of thinking that your purpose in life is to become an expert in some kind of academic subject. But your major in life is about so much more than hitting the books.

For some teens, the goal of being popular surpasses any other goal on their agenda. In the poignant movie *13 Going on 30,* actress Jennifer Garner plays Jenna Rink, who is consumed with her overwhelming desire to be popular. She will do anything to be accepted by the in crowd, even if it means dumping her best friend, Matt, who is not one of the cool thirteen-year-olds. When her wish to become thirty years old is magically fulfilled, she wakes up as a glamorous New York magazine editor. But instead of being ecstatic, as she'd imagined, she's shocked to see where her sacrifices to become popular have led her—she's become a shallow, backstabbing woman with no real friends. Worst of all, she learns she's cut off all communication with her parents and her old buddy Matt.

Of course, in the way of a good movie, she's able to go back in time and correct her mistakes, changing her purpose in life from seeking popularity to just being her real, fantastic self. But you get only one go-around in this life. What will you do with the time you have as a student? Hans Christian Andersen said, "Every man's life is a fairy tale written by God's fingers." The only way for you to find out the life God has for you is to pursue Him with a passion. He says, "You will seek me and find me when you seek me with all your heart" (Jeremiah 29:13 NIV).

The best ways to seek God are through reading His Word and praying to Him. Don't wait until you stand at a fork in the road, needing to make a huge decision. Communicate with Him every moment, replacing your thoughts with His. And the next time someone asks you what your major is, surprise them with the truth: "I'm majoring in loving God and enjoying Him forever." That ought to knock them off their feet!

Purpose
What's Your Major?

What Matters Most...

◎ Reading God's Word. It's how He longs to communicate with you.

◎ Seeking Him in your daily life. Bring Him into your small decisions, not just your big ones.

◎ Majoring in loving Him and enjoying Him forever. That's all that matters.

◎ Giving up your goals in life for His. You'll never be disappointed.

◎ Worshiping Him always. Even when you don't know what's ahead in your future, trust that His plan is good.

What Doesn't Matter...

◎ Knowing what God's will is before you take a step of faith. Your trust springs from hope that He is in control.

◎ Worrying what your friends will think. God's thoughts are so much greater than those of anyone else.

◎ Feeling as if you have it all together. Nobody feels that way deep inside—that's why you must pray for God to help.

◎ Having a definite list of goals for your future. Let them gradually unfold in time.

◎ Taking a step backward every time you take a step forward. Sometimes, life feels that way. One day, you'll look back and see amazing progress.

Focus Points...

I have raised you up for this very purpose, that I might show you my power and that my name might be proclaimed in all the earth.
EXODUS 9:16 NIV

We may make a lot of plans, but the LORD will do what he has decided.
PROVERBS 19:21 CEV

So shall My word be that goes forth from My mouth; it shall not return to Me void, but it shall accomplish what I please, and it shall prosper in the thing for which I sent it.
ISAIAH 55:11 NKJV

The Spirit of God whets our appetite by giving us a taste of what's ahead. He puts a little of heaven in our hearts so that we'll never settle for less.
2 CORINTHIANS 5:5 MSG

what really counts

I shall prepare myself, and my opportunity must come.
ABRAHAM LINCOLN

In the fourth month of life within your mother, your heart suddenly began to beat. Someday, may it be distant, it will beat for the last time. Be sure that the life lived between those beats is lived with meaning and purpose.
NELSON L. PRICE

165

Purpose
One Step at a Time

In his hand is the life of every creature and the breath of all mankind.
JOB 12:10 NIV

what
really
counts

An artist takes a knife and slices off a muddy hunk of clay. It looks like a gray, shapeless blob to you and me, but in her mind, she's seeing a finished product. She begins to shape it slowly with her hands, kneading the clay and making it soft. When she's ready, she puts it on her potter's wheel, splashes on some water, and turns on the power. The clay begins to spin, and she continues the smoothing process. Ahhh . . . at last you can see a vase or bowl beginning to develop.

Human beings, too, are formless blocks of clay until God begins to create them into something He desires. He says, "Like the clay in the potter's hand, so are you in My hand, O house of Israel" (Jeremiah 18:6 NASB). In *Experiencing God*, Henry and Richard Blackaby wrote, "It is not a noble task, being clay. There is no glamour to it, nothing boastwor-thy, except that it is exactly what almighty God is looking for. Compliant, moldable, yielded clay."

When clay is being shaped, it doesn't turn to the potter and say, "Hey, could you smooth me out a bit more here and there, so I can become a nice *objet d'art*? I've always wanted to hang out at the Louvre with those charming Europeans." No, the clay doesn't have any say-so at all in its final product. In the same way that clay bends to the artist, your role is to yield yourself to God's skillful hands and allow Him to refine and mold you.

But you don't have to sit around doing nothing while you're waiting to be shaped. When you were in elementary school, you probably learned that Thomas Edison invented the lightbulb. But do you think he just woke up one day with this brilliant idea? In fact, he didn't learn to talk until he was four years old. He attended formal school for only three months, and his teacher thought his brains were "scrambled" because he asked so many questions. He tried out a dozen careers in different cities before he finally found his calling. Even then, it took years of hard work, trial, and error before Edison began to patent his hundreds of inventions, one of which was the lightbulb. His famous advice still holds true today: "Everything comes to him who hustles while he waits."

Purpose
One Step at a Time

What Matters Most...

- Praying for God to show you His purpose. He will reveal it to you one step at a time.

- Being patient. God is shaping and refining you to fulfill His purpose.

- Renewing your mind. Focus on transforming your thought life to please God.

- Remembering that God is in control of your life. You'll understand a lot more about God's purpose for you a year from now.

- Hustling while you wait. In other words, get busy doing the little things you know you need to be doing, while you wait for the big plan to be revealed.

What Doesn't Matter...

- Your past mistakes. God the Artist can refine and mold you into something new.

- Your personal game plan. It's all about His plan, not yours.

- Your vision of success. Seek God first, and your vision may change to conform with His.

- Your abilities. He will enable you to do that which He has called you to do.

- Your calendar. God does not work according to your time frame; He has His own lifetime planner.

Focus Points...

We know that God causes all things to work together for good to those who love God, to those who are called according to His purpose.
ROMANS 8:28 NASB

The scripture says to Pharaoh, "I have raised you up for the very purpose of showing my power in you, so that my name may be proclaimed in all the earth."
ROMANS 9:17 NRSV

If we have troubles, it is for your comfort and salvation, and if we have comfort, you also have comfort. This helps you to accept patiently the same sufferings we have.
2 CORINTHIANS 1:6 NCV

Now, up on your feet—I have a job for you. I've handpicked you to be a servant and witness to what's happened today, and to what I am going to show you.
ACTS 26:16 MSG

what really counts

Never think that God's delays are God's denials. Hold on; hold fast; hold out. Patience is genius.
GEORGES-LOUIS LECLERC, COMTE DE BUFFON

There is nothing quite as potent as a focused life, one lived on purpose. The men and women who have made the greatest difference in history were the most focused.
RICK WARREN

What Matters Most to Me About
Purpose

God created you with an intense desire to know Him personally, and your main purpose in life is to worship and enjoy Him. You can take steps now to be active in fulfilling His desires for you.

◎ *What are some major things that are burning on your heart right now, that you'd really like to place before the Lord?*

_____

_____

_____

_____

what really counts

_____

_____

_____

◎ *What are some different ways you can express praise to God today?*

_____

_____

_____

_____

_____

_____

_____

◎ *Read Isaiah 64:8. In what ways do you feel that you are clay being shaped by the Potter?*

_____

_____

_____

_____

_____

_____

_____

_____

_____

◎ *Can you name anyone—a friend, a member of your family, or someone famous—who has changed gradually over time to fulfill a more noble purpose?*

_____

_____

_____

_____

_____

_____

_____

_____

_____

O God, Thou hast made us for Thyself, and our hearts are restless until they find their rest in Thee.

SAINT AUGUSTINE

HAPPINESS

An Introduction

> You will keep in perfect peace him whose mind is steadfast, because he trusts in you.
>
> ISAIAH 26:3 NIV

what really counts

How far will you go to feel happy? In the Declaration of Independence, Thomas Jefferson listed the "pursuit of happiness" among Americans' "inalienable rights." You may feel that the world owes it to you; after all, you work hard, and you lead a busy life. When you look around you, marketers bombard you with the message that you need to pay them for their product, and then you'll be happy. You may not realize it, but you're heavily targeted by marketing think tanks that were created with the goal of learning how members of the under-thirty generation think and spend.

And it seems to be working. Every year, U.S. teens spend $172 billion on "stuff"—technological gadgets, clothes, music, food, and entertainment. But does it bring you happiness? Being happy is based on external circumstances that you often have no control over. If you have a good day, you feel happy. But the next day, something drags you down into a slump. Helen Keller said, "Many people have a wrong idea of what constitutes true happiness. It is not attained through self-gratification, but through fidelity to a worthy purpose."

The only lasting joy and peace come from knowing God and finding His goals for your life. When you learn to do this, you can be one of those people who lead others to Christ because you've learned the secret to true joy and peace. It's a heart thing that all begins with a prayer of thanks.

> How completely satisfying to turn from our limitations to a God who has none ... God never hurries. There are no deadlines against which he must work. To know this is to quiet our spirits and relax our nerves.
>
> A. W. TOZER

Happiness
Quit Your Whining

Always be joyful. Keep on praying. No matter what happens, always be thankful, for this is God's will for you who belong to Christ Jesus.

1 Thessalonians 5:16–18 NLT

what really counts

Have you ever been in a grocery store and overheard a cranky kid whining to his parent about something he wants? "I want it, Mommy! I need it, Daddy!" he shouts, pointing to a rack full of candy or cheap plastic toys. Maybe you've seen him screaming on the floor with his legs kicking in the air, like a bug turned over on its back. It's the most annoying sound in the world, isn't it? But be honest: Do you ever whine like that to God?

As a student, it's easy to feel as if you have too much to do and too little time to do it. You complain a little—maybe to a friend, to your parents, or to your boss. It's easy to turn those complaints toward God, as you find yourself with a bad case of the "if only's." *If only* I had more time, I could get all my work done and make good grades. *If only* I had more money, I could buy everything I really need. *If only* I lived in a different house, or in a different city. *If only* I were some other age.

The surest cure for whining is to count your blessings. You have so much to be thankful for. The very fact that you are alive and breathing is a gift. Can you walk? Can you talk? Can you see? Did you sleep in a bed last night? It's easy to take those kinds of things for granted.

Everybody complains sometimes and forgets to be grateful. Think of the Israelites as they wandered for forty years through the desert. God punished them for their hearts of ingratitude. Sure, you might be thinking, *I'd complain too if I were stumbling around a hot desert, living in a tent, and eating manna every day.* But it was their attitude of haste and forgetfulness that angered God. He wanted them to remember all He had done for them, in allowing them to escape their four hundred years of cruel slavery to the Egyptians. You think of forgetfulness as a harmless weakness—something professors and old people have to worry about. But when you forget the blessings of God, the results can be quite serious; it can cause you to trade your happiness for whining and ingratitude. Remembering what God has done for you in the past is the surest way to turn a whining attitude into a heart of joy and praise.

Happiness
Quit Your Whining

What Matters Most...

- Cultivating an attitude of gratitude. It's the surest cure for a bad case of the "if only's."

- Remembering the good things God has done for you and for others in the past.

- Finding creative ways to thank Him, through sharing, prayer, and praise.

- Living in the here and now, and not wishing you could be someplace else.

- Focusing on positive thoughts and blocking out the negative ones with Scripture.

What Doesn't Matter...

- Broken promises. People aren't perfect, but God is. He promises He will "never leave you nor forsake you" (Deuteronomy 31:6 NIV).

- Broken dreams. Give them to God, and let Him create something new and fresh for your life.

- Broken hearts. It helps to remember that Jesus, too, suffered and felt rejected while He was on earth.

- Broken plans. When you seek first God's kingdom, you may find out that your original plans were not His best for you.

- Broken people. Sometimes, the only way God can get your attention is to take away the things you idolize.

Focus Points...

Give thanks to the LORD, call upon His name; make known His deeds among the peoples.
1 CHRONICLES 16:8 NASB

Let us be thankful, then, because we receive a kingdom that cannot be shaken. Let us be grateful and worship God in a way that will please him, with reverence and awe.
HEBREWS 12:28 GNT

Our Lord and God, you are worthy to receive glory, honor, and power. You created all things, and by your decision they are and were created.
REVELATION 4:11 CEV

By contrast, the fruit of the Spirit is love, joy, peace, patience, kindness, generosity, faithfulness, gentleness, and self-control. There is no law against such things.
GALATIANS 5:22–23 NRSV

what really counts

The most valuable thing the psalms do for me is to express the same delight in God which made David dance.
C. S. LEWIS

Trust in yourself and you are doomed to disappointment... but trust in GOD, and you are never to be confounded in time or eternity.
DWIGHT L. MOODY

Happiness
Right Here, Right Now

> Take delight in the LORD, and He
> will give you your heart's desires.
> PSALM 37:4 HCSB

When you're in the eighth grade, you look at all the high schoolers and think, *I can't wait to be in high school.* Then you're a freshman, and you find yourself wishing you could be a cool sophomore. Soon you begin to think life begins when you're an upperclassman, and then you're champing at the bit to get off to college. It doesn't stop there. Maybe you get a bum roommate, and you can't wait to live with someone new. Then you meet the love of your life, and you think you will die if you can't be married.

Although this is how many people live, it's not what pleases God. When you spend your time wishing your life away, you miss out on the pure joy of living in the now. David was probably leaping for joy when he wrote these words: "I inherited your book on living; it's mine forever—what a gift! And how happy it makes me!" (Psalm 119:111 MSG). He learned that the secret of being joyful is meditating on God's

Word. By dwelling on God's perfection and perfect love, you can learn to appreciate the gifts He's given you. In doing so, you'll be able to praise God no matter what your circumstances.

Do you remember the children's book *Alexander and the Terrible, Horrible, No-Good, Very Bad Day*? Poor Alexander— he wakes up with gum in his hair, he trips on his skateboard when he gets out of bed, and he drops his sweater into the sink full of water. His day moves from bad to worse as he gets smushed in his car pool, finds out he has a cavity, and sees kissing on television. Alexander concludes that the only way out of a day like this is to move to Australia.

But there's a better way! More than three hundred years ago in France, a man named Nicholas Herman entered a monastery and was put to work in the kitchen, washing dishes and cooking. What could have been considered drudgery to some became a place where this man began to learn to continually practice the presence of God. He has become known throughout the world as Brother Lawrence, and his methods of prayer have encouraged millions. He wrote, "There is not in the world a kind of life more sweet and delightful than that of a continual conversation with God." This is true happiness, right here, right now.

Happiness
Right Here, Right Now

What Matters Most...

◎ Practicing a continual conversation with God, telling Him your thoughts and feelings.

◎ Trusting God that He will lead you in the right direction, even when you're not sure where you're going.

◎ Being patient as you wait for the treasures of each day to be opened to you.

◎ Looking for God all around you—in nature, in people, in His Word.

◎ Sharing good moments with others so they can rejoice with you.

What Doesn't Matter...

◎ Wishing you could be in a new phase of life or living someplace else. Be content right here, right now.

◎ Feeling as if you don't have a reason to praise God. Dig deep, and be thankful.

◎ Focusing on external circumstances. That's not where peace and lasting happiness lie.

◎ Worrying about the future. Tomorrow is out of your control, but your attitude today is not.

◎ Thinking you'll be happy once you get through this *thing* you're going through. Learn to cultivate joy as a way of life.

Focus Points...

A heart at peace gives life to the body, but envy rots the bones.
PROVERBS 14:30 NIV

Look at those who are honest and good, for a wonderful future lies before those who love peace.
PSALM 37:37 NLT

Depart from evil and do good; seek peace and pursue it.
PSALM 34:14 NKJV

Now that we have been put right with God through faith, we have peace with God through our Lord Jesus Christ.
ROMANS 5:1 GNT

I'm leaving you peace. I'm giving you my peace. I don't give you the kind of peace that the world gives. So don't be troubled or cowardly.
JOHN 14:27 GOD'S WORD

what really counts

If our minds are stayed upon God, His peace will rule the affairs entertained by our minds. If, on the other hand, we allow our minds to dwell on the cares of this world, God's peace will be far from our thoughts.

WOODROLL KROLL

The secret of happiness is not in doing what one likes, but in liking what one has to do.

J. M. BARRIE

What Matters Most to Me About
Happiness

You cannot find true peace and happiness in what's going on around you. It's up to you to make sure that godly wisdom fills your thoughts and attitudes. The first step you can take toward having a good attitude is to be thankful.

◉ *Look at 1 Peter 3:11. What does this verse tell you to turn away from? What are you commanded to do?*

_____

_____

_____

_____

_____

_____

_____

_____

◉ *Have you ever had a day when something good happened and you felt really happy? What about the opposite? How can you find joy that is not based on your circumstances?*

_____

_____

_____

_____

_____

_____

_____

◉ *Do you ever feel like you are whining to God? What about? Can you turn those complaints into gratitude? What are some things you are thankful for today?*

_____

_____

_____

_____

_____

_____

_____

_____

◉ *Name two things about the life of Christ that demonstrate His attitude of joyfulness despite difficult circumstances. What can you learn from Him?*

_____

_____

_____

_____

_____

_____

_____

_____

_____

To the man who pleases him, God gives
wisdom, knowledge and happiness.
ECCLESIASTES 2:26 NIV

PERSONAL GROWTH

An Introduction

> Work out your own salvation with fear and trembling; for it is God who works in you both to will and to do for His good pleasure.
>
> PHILIPPIANS 2:12–13 NKJV

what really counts

God loves you just the way you are. That's the great miracle of the gospel. And yet, He doesn't leave you the way you are. He is constantly molding you into the person you were born to be. He's making you look more like Christ. And in order to do that, He requires some help from you. Sure, God could just touch you on the forehead and *Zap!* you'll suddenly be holy. But that's not the way God has chosen to make your righteousness happen.

Just as your body gets stronger through working out, so does your character. You are called to work out your salvation. You can't work for your salvation; the Bible is very clear about that. But you do have to work it out. As you exercise your spiritual muscles, they will grow stronger. If you are in Christ, God has declared you to be righteous. Now is the time to put that spiritual reality into practice in your daily life.

A Christlike life is one of freedom—freedom to pursue your deepest desires, freedom to be gracious and forgiving toward other people, freedom to be yourself. It's a life marked by confidence, integrity, and a willingness to take responsibility for your own actions. It takes work to become that kind of person. But it's worth it. And it's not out of reach, because in the end, it's really God who's at work when you work out your salvation, shaping your life into one that pleases Him.

Jesus, like any good fisherman, first catches the fish; then he cleans them.

MARK POTTER

Personal Growth
Long-Term Vision

> [The righteous] are strong, like a tree
> planted by a river. The tree produces
> fruit in season, and its leaves don't die.
> Everything they do will succeed.
>
> PSALM 1:3 NCV

what really counts

Before he became president of the United States, James Garfield was the principal of Hiram College. One day the father of one of Garfield's students came to ask if his son's course of study could be altered to allow him to complete his degree requirements sooner. "Certainly," Garfield answered. "But it all depends on what you want to make of your boy. When God wants to make an oak tree, He takes a hundred years. But when He wants to make a squash, He requires only two months."

You're an oak tree, not a squash. It takes a long time to become what God wants you to be. He wants you to be a person of strength and stability. That's what you want for yourself, no doubt. But there are no shortcuts to maturity. That's why it's so important for you to have a long-term vision for your life. What kind of person do you want to be in ten years? In twenty years? You make decisions every day of your life, some big, many small. What are you going to wear? With whom are you going to spend your time? What are you going to major in? Are you going to study or go to a party? With every decision, ask yourself if you are making a step toward the person you want to become.

There's a tension in the Bible between keeping long-term vision and not taking the future for granted. Many verses encourage you to consider your children and your children's children when you make decisions; that's very long-term thinking when you aren't even married yet. But then there are other verses that suggest it's unwise to make too many plans for the future, since nobody really knows what it holds. The balance between the two views comes in passages like Proverbs 4:25–26: "Let your eyes look directly ahead and let your gaze be fixed straight in front of you. Watch the path of your feet and all your ways will be established" (NASB). Look straight ahead, eyes to the future. But as you do that, look to your feet, making one step at a time.

Long-term vision, short-term focus. That's the secret to living for the long haul. Tend to your business today; do what you know you're supposed to be doing today. And you'll find that you've grown strong and stable, like an oak tree. Just keep moving forward, one step at a time.

Personal Growth
Long-Term Vision

What Matters Most...

◎ The work of God in your life. He knows what He is doing.

◎ Oakishness. The oak grows slowly—a hundred years—but it grows strong.

◎ God's timing. It's perfect. He knows exactly how long will produce the best results.

◎ Deep roots. Go deep into the things of God.

◎ Rich soil. Prayer and Scripture nourish your roots. Saturate yourself in both.

What Doesn't Matter...

◎ Your timing. You can rest in God's work, however slow it seems.

◎ Your mistakes. You don't become godly all at once.

◎ Quick solutions. They don't usually work and often end up taking twice the time.

◎ Other people's opinions. God is at work in your life, and His is the only opinion that matters.

◎ The feeling that you'll never get there. God finishes what He starts.

Focus Points...

Good people will prosper like palm trees, grow tall like Lebanon cedars; transplanted to GOD's courtyard, they'll grow tall in the presence of God, lithe and green, virile still in old age.
PSALM 92:12–14 MSG

See how the farmer waits for the precious fruit of the earth, waiting patiently for it until it receives the early and latter rain.
JAMES 5:7 NKJV

Don't try to get out of anything prematurely. Let it do its work so you become mature and well-developed, not deficient in any way.
JAMES 1:4 MSG

what
really
counts

Endings are better than beginnings. Sticking to it is better than standing out.
ECCLESIASTES 7:8 MSG

He who waits on God never waits too long.
CHUCK WAGNER

Taken separately, the experiences of life can work harm and not good. Taken together, they make a pattern of blessing and strength the like of which the world does not know.
V. RAYMOND BROWN

Personal Growth
You Are What You Think

> Be careful what you think, because
> your thoughts run your life.
> PROVERBS 4:23 NCV

You've probably seen pictures or figurines of the Three Little Monkeys—See No Evil, Hear No Evil, and Speak No Evil. See no evil. Hear no evil. Speak no evil. That's pretty good advice if you can manage it. You can probably think of ways you could see and hear less evil—by switching off the television, monitoring what Web sites you visit, staying out of places you know you shouldn't be. But *no* evil? You live in a world where evil is real. You're going to see and hear it.

The Three Little Monkeys offer a view of right living that's based on what you shouldn't do, what you should stay away from. The Bible offers a different view: "Summing it all up, friends, I'd say you'll do best by filling your minds and meditating on things true, noble, reputable, authentic, compelling, gracious—the best, not the worst; the beautiful, not the ugly; things to praise, not things to curse" (Philippians 4:8 MSG). The Three Little Monkeys tell you what to avoid. The

Bible calls you to fill your mind with so many good things that even when evil can't be avoided, it won't find a place in your mind to perch.

Do you want to guard your heart from evil? You've heard the slogan "Just say no." Fine. But you'd better say yes to something better. Dwell on the beautiful, the true, the noble, and let it work itself into your life. Think the best of others, not the worst. Dwell on their beauties, not their failures. Fill your mind with the Word of God. That's your true defense against the lies you hear—a mind and heart so full of truth that falsehood rolls right off.

You live from the inside out. Jesus said it's not what comes in from the outside that corrupts a person, but what comes out from the inside. It's important to control what you take in as much as possible. See as little evil as possible. Hear as little evil as possible. But unless you plan to lock yourself in a closet, you can't prevent all evil from coming at you from the outside. And even if you did lock yourself in a closet, you'd find out that you still have your thought life to deal with. That's where the real action is. That's the true challenge. But it's also the place where you have the most control. And that's good news.

Personal Growth
You Are What You Think

What Matters Most...

◎ Your inner life. This is where your outward life begins, in your heart and in your soul.

◎ Your beliefs. They need to line up with God's Word.

◎ Your desires. They need to line up with God's desires for you.

◎ A mind full of what's good, true, honest, and noble. Leave no room for evil in your mind.

◎ An outward life that reflects your inner life. Be real.

What Doesn't Matter...

◎ Putting up a good front. God looks at the heart.

◎ Past hypocrisy. You can make a new start no matter how you've acted in the past.

◎ The unavoidable. Control what you can control, and trust God to protect your mind and heart from the negatives you can't control.

◎ Unrealistic expectations. "See no evil" is impossible. "See *less* evil"—that's a workable plan.

◎ Self-punishment. Focus on filling your mind with good things, not punishing yourself for your shortcomings.

Focus Points...

What people say with their mouths comes from the way they think; these are the things that make people unclean. Out of the mind come evil thoughts, murder, adultery, sexual sins, stealing, lying, and speaking evil of others. These things make people unclean; eating with unwashed hands does not make them unclean.
MATTHEW 15:18–20 NCV

The thoughts of the righteous are right, but the counsels of the wicked are deceitful.
PROVERBS 12:5 NKJV

When I remember You on my bed, I meditate on You in the night watches.
PSALM 63:6 NKJV

A good man out of the good treasure of his heart brings forth good; and an evil man out of the evil treasure of his heart brings forth evil. For out of the abundance of the heart his mouth speaks.
LUKE 6:45 NKJV

What we plant in the soil of contemplation, we shall reap in the harvest of action.

MEISTER ECKHART

Man's mind is a watch that needs winding daily.

WELSH PROVERB

193

Personal Growth
Real Confidence

> Therefore do not cast away your confidence, which has great reward.
> HEBREWS 10:35 NKJV

You're fifty feet in the air, standing on a limb. You don't dare look down. A fall from here would . . . you don't even want to think about what a fall from here would do. Your assignment is to jump out to a rope that will let you swing to the next tree, but you've never jumped that far before. At least you've never jumped that far when you were fifty feet off the ground. But you decide to face your fears. You swallow hard and make the leap. And you make it. You soar like Tarzan from tree to tree, and it's exhilarating.

If you've ever done a high-ropes course, you know what a confidence-builder it is to go beyond your limits and find out you could do things you didn't know you could do. But if you've ever done a high-ropes course, you also know what makes it possible for you to stretch your limits when you're fifty feet in the air: the safety line. It's because of your confidence in the safety line that you can have the self-confidence to make the leap at that dizzying height. Without the safety line, it would be pure insanity. Does that mean the self-confidence you feel on a ropes course is false? Of course not. It just means that your self-confidence was made possible by a confidence in something strong and sure that was outside yourself.

Life can be like a high-ropes course. Sometimes it takes confidence in a strength and surety outside yourself. The basis of your confidence is the God who is always faithful. Your strength ebbs and flows. Your wisdom and judgment are sometimes better, sometimes not so good. But God never changes. A confidence in the God who will never let you fall all the way to the ground makes it possible for you to stretch yourself, to do things you never thought you could do.

Self-confidence is a good thing, as far as it goes. It's certainly a whole lot better than wallowing in self-pity and low self-esteem. But confidence that doesn't reach beyond itself is fragile. The confidence that really changes your life is a confidence in the God who is utterly trustworthy. The self-esteem that lasts is based on the esteem that God holds you in. You have plenty of reasons to be self-confident, and they all grow out of a confidence in God.

Personal Growth
Real Confidence

What Matters Most...

- ◉ God's trustworthiness. He never fails.

- ◉ A self-confidence that is based on a confidence in God. That's confidence that can stand the test.

- ◉ A self-image that's based on God's image of you. That's real self-esteem.

- ◉ Stretching your limits. God's there to catch you if you overdo it.

- ◉ The exhilaration of living beyond what you thought you could do. Why be average?

What **Doesn't** Matter...

- ◉ A false self-image. God delights in you for who you are.

- ◉ Fear of falling. God is your safety rope.

- ◉ Self-reliance. Rely on God's strength.

- ◉ Playing it safe. You never know what you can be until you step out in faith.

- ◉ Your limits. As you place your confidence in God, you find out your limits aren't what you thought they were.

Focus Points...

It is better to take refuge in the LORD than to trust in nobles.
PSALM 118:9 HCSB

I am confident of this very thing, that He who began a good work in you will perfect it until the day of Christ Jesus.
PHILIPPIANS 1:6 NASB

This is the confidence that we have in Him, that if we ask anything according to His will, He hears us.
1 JOHN 5:14 NKJV

Little children, abide in Him, that when He appears, we may have confidence and not be ashamed before Him at His coming.
1 JOHN 2:28 NKJV

The LORD will be your confidence, and will keep your foot from being caught.
PROVERBS 3:26 NKJV

what really counts

Religion is the possibility of the removal of every ground of confidence except confidence in God alone.

KARL BARTH

The ultimate ground of faith and knowledge is confidence in God.

CHARLES HODGE

Personal Growth
Desire

> Delight yourself also in the LORD,
> and He shall give you the desires
> of your heart.
>
> PSALM 37:4 NKJV

what really counts

What do you want? When you've answered that question, take it one level deeper. If you were to get what you say you want, what need do you think that would fulfill? Because that's what you really want. You want to be valedictorian, but what you really want is to feel the self-worth that goes along with that kind of accomplishment, or to make your parents proud. You want a lot of money, but what you really want is to feel secure and important. You want a boyfriend or girlfriend, but what you really want is to feel loved.

Your deepest desires are pointing you toward God, the only Being in the universe who can fulfill them. Your worth is found in Him. Your acceptance is found in Him too, and your security. And your need to be loved is met by the God who is love. All those needs you feel are like homing signals, pointing you back toward the God who gave you life. There's a God-shaped hole in every person's soul, as the French philosopher Blaise Pascal noted. And no matter what you try to fill that hole with, the only thing that will plug it is God Himself.

The problem, of course, is that you have lots of desires, and many of them conflict with your deepest desires, or at least throw you off their track. You desire to be entertained. You desire thrills. You desire to sleep until noon on Sundays. And any of those desires, you can argue, is just a smaller version—or a twisted version—of those deeper desires. The desire to please other people is just a paler version of the desire to be accepted for who you are. The desire for casual sex is a crippled version of the desire for intimacy. The problem, as C. S. Lewis put it, isn't that you desire too much, but that you desire too little. And if you're not careful, you can be like the undisciplined bird dog who lets the pheasant fly away while he's chasing lizards and grasshoppers.

God loves you. He wants to give you the desires of your heart. In fact, He alone can. The key to a godly life isn't to curb all your desires. The key is to recognize what your deepest desires really are and to turn them loose to lead you to the God who can fulfill them.

Personal Growth
Desire

What Matters Most...

◎ Knowing what you really want. That takes real discernment.

◎ Not letting smaller desires throw you off the scent of what you really desire. Let your desires lead you to their ultimate source.

◎ Following your desires to the God who can fulfill them. He's the only desire that's worthy of you.

◎ Wanting more, not less. Don't settle for mediocrity.

◎ Asking God for judgment to distinguish between true and false desires. Sometimes it's hard to tell on your own.

What Doesn't Matter...

◎ Lesser desires. They can make you lose sight of what is greater.

◎ Apathy. It can keep you from pursuing what you really want.

◎ The mistaken belief that if it feels good, you should do it. Sometimes the right thing doesn't feel good at first.

◎ The equally mistaken belief that all desire is bad. It's not selfish to go after what you want—as long as your desires are in line with God's.

◎ The world's desires. Take your cues from God.

Focus Points...

You open Your hand and satisfy the desire of every living thing.
PSALM 145:16 NKJV

[People] start worrying about the needs of this life. They are fooled by the desire to get rich and to have all kinds of other things. So the message gets choked out, and they never produce anything.
MARK 4:19 CEV

Those who are Christ's have crucified the flesh with its passions and desires.
GALATIANS 5:24 NKJV

I say, walk by the Spirit, and you will not carry out the desire of the flesh.
GALATIANS 5:16 NASB

what really counts

All men seek happiness. This is without exception. Whatever different means they employ, they all tend to this end. The cause of some going to war, and of others avoiding it, is the same desire in both, attended with different views.

BLAISE PASCAL

Christ is not valued at all unless He is valued above all.
SAINT AUGUSTINE

Personal Growth
Freeing Others, Freeing Yourself

> Be even-tempered, content with second place,
> quick to forgive an offense. Forgive as quickly
> and completely as the Master forgave you.
>
> COLOSSIANS 3:13 MSG

what really counts

You hear a *splat!* on the front porch, followed by the squeal of tires on pavement. Running out the front door you see the flash of taillights disappearing beyond the stop sign. Then you notice the broken eggshells on the threshold and the sticky egg whites and yolks sliding down the front door. You've been egged. You feel violated. You get a spatula and scrape up as much egg as you can and put it in a can. You look at the shattered shells and ruptured yolks sadly suspended in the dirty white, and it burns you up to think that someone would do such a thing.

You start to throw the broken eggs away, but for some reason you don't. You leave them out on the counter. You look at them the next morning when you come down for breakfast, and you get mad all over again at the thought that somebody would egg your house. But you still don't throw the eggs away. You leave them on the counter as a reminder of the anger and hurt you felt the night before. After a few days, the eggs begin to smell. That makes you even madder: Now those vandals have stunk up your house! Before long the eggs turn green with rot, and your house stinks so badly that none of your friends will set foot in your house. Now, you fume, those egg-throwers have ruined your social life, too.

It's a ridiculous scenario, isn't it? Nobody in his right mind would leave eggs out on the counter to spoil and rot. And yet refusing to forgive another person who has wronged you isn't very different. By holding on to another person's sin, you might think you're holding them hostage in some way. Unforgiveness might feel like a kind of revenge. But the truth is, you're the one being held hostage if you don't forgive. You're the one living with rotting eggs. But it's a captivity you can free yourself from. Just let go of the anger and hurt. Forgive. Throw away the rotten eggs.

Somebody has said that refusing to forgive is like drinking poison and expecting another person to get sick. When God forgave you, He set you free. Now you have the freedom to free people who have wronged you. More than that, you have the freedom to set yourself free.

Personal Growth
Freeing Others, Freeing Yourself

What Matters Most...

- The forgiveness you have received from God. This is your motivation to forgive others.

- A loving spirit. Love doesn't keep track of wrongs.

- Keeping yourself free. Don't throw away your freedom by enslaving yourself to bitterness.

- Freeing others. You need not try to punish other people's wrongs

- Keeping a clear conscience. Ask forgiveness of anyone you've wronged.

What Doesn't Matter...

- The desire for payback. Being free is better than getting back.

- The size of the wrong that was done. Big or small, your best bet is to let it go.

- How long ago it happened. Years ago, or earlier today, now's the time to forgive.

- Whose fault it is. Don't keep a ledger.

- Pride. Would you willingly enslave yourself for pride's sake?

Focus Points...

Forgive us our debts, as we forgive our debtors.
MATTHEW 6:12 NKJV

You're well-known as good and forgiving, bighearted to all who ask for help.
PSALM 86:5 MSG

If he sins against you seven times in a day, and seven times in a day returns to you, saying, "I repent," you shall forgive him.
LUKE 17:4 NKJV

Happy is the person whose sins are forgiven, whose wrongs are pardoned.
PSALM 32:1 NCV

what really counts

Whenever you stand praying, if you have anything against anyone, forgive him, that your Father in heaven may also forgive you your trespasses.
MARK 11:25 NKJV

Forgiveness does not mean ignoring what has been done or putting a false label on an evil act. It means, rather, that the evil act no longer remains as a barrier to the relationship.

MARTIN LUTHER KING JR.

To carry a grudge is like being stung to death by one bee.
WILLIAM H. WALTON

Personal Growth
Taking Responsibility

> With your whole being you embrace God setting things right, and then you say it, right out loud: "God has set everything right between him and me!"
>
> ROMANS 10:10 MSG

The goat stands in the slanting light of autumn, bug-eyed and skittish at the sight of so many people watching it so intently. It strains against its rope, shrinking away from the priest in his heavy, ornate robes. The priest's hands are on the goat's head now, and he speaks in a loud voice that carries across the temple courtyard, confessing the sins of the Jewish people on this high and holy day, the Day of Atonement. The sins of the people have now been symbolically transferred to the head of the bewildered goat, and when the rope is released from around its neck, it tears out across the courtyard, down the little aisle where the people have parted to make a way for it, through the streets of Jerusalem, and out into the wilderness beyond. The poor goat—the scapegoat—doesn't stop running until it is out in the desert, far from the people whose sins it carries, never to return.

The term *scapegoat* is still in common use, but it means something very different from what it meant for the ancient Israelites. Nowadays, a scapegoat is a person who gets blamed for something that somebody else has done. If you've done wrong and you figure out a way to shift the blame to your little brother, that's scapegoating. That's human nature for you—anything to keep from admitting you're wrong. Better to find a scapegoat to blame.

That's not what the ancient scapegoat ritual was about, however. It was about taking responsibility for your mistakes and failures, and in so doing, sending them away never to trouble you again. On the Day of Atonement every year, the people of Israel didn't say, "We're innocent; the goat did it!" Instead, they said, "We have done many things wrong, as we acknowledge by symbolically placing those wrongs on the head of this goat. Now, merciful God, please send our wrongs away just as we send this goat into the wilderness."

The scapegoat is a picture of Christ, who took on His own head everything you wish you had never done. He carries all those faults, all those wrongs away so they can't hurt you anymore. Do you want to be free? Don't go looking for someone to blame for your shortcomings. Own them. Admit to them. Then let Jesus, the divine scapegoat, carry them far away from you.

Personal Growth
Taking Responsibility

What Matters Most...

- ◎ Taking responsibility for your actions. It's the only way to move on.

- ◎ Clearing the slate. Don't let wrongs pile up.

- ◎ Starting fresh. Keep moving upward. Live right.

- ◎ Living with integrity. Free yourself from false fronts.

- ◎ Living in the present. The past is past. The future is bright for those who live with a clear conscience in the present.

What Doesn't Matter...

- ◎ The wrongs you've done. If you take responsibility, Christ removes them from you.

- ◎ The instinct to blame others. The only scapegoat you need is Christ.

- ◎ The instinct to hide your imperfections. Be open with God and others.

- ◎ Your shortcomings. Take responsibility for those, too. God is still working on you.

- ◎ Feelings of guilt. God forgives those who own up to their sins.

Focus Points...

You can't whitewash your sins and get by with it; you find mercy by admitting and leaving them.
PROVERBS 28:13 MSG

Each of us shall give account of himself to God.
ROMANS 14:12 NKJV

It's easy to see a smudge on your neighbor's face and be oblivious to the ugly sneer on your own. Do you have the nerve to say, "Let me wash your face for you," when your own face is distorted by contempt?
MATTHEW 7:3–4 MSG

If you think you can judge others, you are wrong. When you judge them, you are really judging yourself guilty, because you do the same things they do.
ROMANS 2:1 NCV

what really counts

The price of greatness is responsibility.

WINSTON CHURCHILL

One of the annoying things about believing in free will and individual responsibility is the difficulty in finding someone to blame your troubles on. And when you do find someone, it's remarkable how often their picture turns up on you driver's license.

P. J. O'ROURKE

Personal Growth
People Pleasing

Whether we are at home with the Lord or away from him, we still try our best to please him.

2 CORINTHIANS 5:9 CEV

what really counts

"Think differently." You've probably seen the ads featuring people whose unique vision changed the world—people like Martin Luther King Jr. and Muhammad Ali. By bringing a new perspective to bear on the world around them, these people gave everybody a new way to see things. Because they thought differently, other people began to think differently too. The people who have a real impact—for better or for worse—are the people who choose not to think, act, and look like the world around them.

"Do not change yourselves to be like the people of this world, but be changed within by a new way of thinking. Then you will be able to decide what God wants for you; you will know what is good and pleasing to him and what is perfect" (Romans 12:2 NCV). You're called to think differently too. You're called to bring the mind of Christ to bear on your school, your job, your family, your friendships, your dating relationships—all of life. That's what pleases God. And in the end it's what pleases you, too, for it's the only way to stay true to yourself.

Changing yourself might seem like the easy thing to do. You may have heard the saying "Go along to get along." Here's the problem with that plan. You go along to get along today. But tomorrow you're going to have to go along with something else if you still want to get along. People change, and if you change yourself just to please them, it's not long before you've gotten so far from your real self that you don't remember who you are. Jesus said you can't serve two masters. If you want to please God, you can't shape your life around pleasing other people.

You may be thinking, *That sounds good, but won't that make me look like a freak?* Maybe. You may find yourself in situations where people treat you like an outcast if you choose to please God instead of pleasing them. But the rewards of a God-pleasing life far outweigh the rewards of a temporary popularity bought with your unique selfhood. And you may find that you aren't treated as an outcast after all. Proverbs 16:7 says, "When people live so that they please the LORD, even their enemies will make peace with them" (NCV). Think differently. You might change the world.

Personal Growth
People Pleasing

What Matters Most...

- Pleasing God. That should be your ambition.

- Being true to who God made you to be. That's the real you.

- Leading by example and not following the herd. Choose not to think, act, and look like everyone else in the world.

- Thinking differently from the people around you. You're unique.

- Changing the world. It's not too much to ask.

What Doesn't Matter...

- Following the latest fad. You only need to follow Christ.

- Pleasing others. Their tastes change too quickly to keep up.

- Fitting in. If you're true to yourself, you'll probably stand out.

- Other people's agendas for you. God's agenda is what matters.

- Other people's opinions of you. How well do they really know you?

Focus Points...

God was pleased to trust us with his message. We didn't speak to please people, but to please God who knows our motives.
1 THESSALONIANS 2:4 CEV

Do I now persuade men, or God? Or do I seek to please men? For if I still pleased men, I would not be a bondservant of Christ.
GALATIANS 1:10 NKJV

Your task is to single-mindedly serve Christ. Do that and you'll kill two birds with one stone: pleasing the God above you and proving your worth to the people around you.
ROMANS 14:18 MSG

Brothers and sisters, we taught you how to live in a way that will please God, and you are living that way. Now we ask and encourage you in the Lord Jesus to live that way even more.
1 THESSALONIANS 4:1 NCV

what really counts

If you seek first to please God and are satisfied therein, you have but one to please instead of multitudes; and a multitude of masters are hardlier pleased than one.

RICHARD BAXTER

I don't know the key to success, but the key to failure is trying to please everybody.

BILL COSBY

Personal Growth
Gracious Goodness

> Because of the kindness that God has shown me, I ask you not to think of yourselves more highly than you should. Instead, your thoughts should lead you to use good judgment based on what God has given each of you as believers.
>
> ROMANS 12:3 GOD'S WORD

what really counts

Young David arrived at the battlefield bearing a care package—fresh-baked bread and roasted grain, a little taste of home for his older brothers, who had been eating army rations for more than a month. Imagine David's surprise when his eldest brother, Eliab, exploded in rage: "Why did you come down here? . . . I know your arrogance and your evil heart—you came down to see the battle." You can hear the hurt in David's voice, his astonishment that Eliab would ascribe such terrible motives to him: " 'What have I done now?' protested David. 'It was just a question' " (1 Samuel 16:28–29 HCSB).

Eliab's reaction seems strange and out of proportion. But consider his situation. For forty days in a row, Goliath had stepped onto the battlefield to challenge and taunt the fighting men of Israel. Every day, the Israelites shrank in fear, and every day they believed the giant's insults a little more. For forty days in a row Eliab, like the rest of the Israelites, had been reminded of his own weakness and cowardice. Think what that would do to your self-image, and maybe you can better understand Eliab's strange response—even if you can't justify it.

You may have noticed that the people who are the hardest on others are often those who feel the worst about themselves. It's when a person feels like an idiot that he or she is most likely to call another person stupid. It's when a person feels guilty that he or she is most likely to condemn another person's mistakes. But Jesus sets you free from all that. When He looks at you, He doesn't see your faults and shortcomings. He sees the real you—the one whom He is shaping into His own image. He cherishes you as His own, and in His grace He sets you free from your feelings of unworthiness and shame. He gives you a new way to look at yourself. And that means He gives you a new way to look at others.

David's brother Eliab felt so worthless that he believed his only hope of feeling better was to make someone else feel worse. But your self-worth derives from the God who thought well enough of you to die for you. When God's grace sinks into your life, it changes the way you live. You're free from self-punishment, and you learn to set people free rather than punishing them.

Personal Growth
Gracious Goodness

What Matters Most...

◎ God's grace in your life. He's doing great things in you.

◎ God's grace in other people's lives. There's your motivation to be gracious.

◎ A new you. You have a whole new way of looking at things and people.

◎ Forgiveness. You've been forgiven, so you can forgive others.

◎ The benefit of the doubt. Since you don't know anybody else's motives, you might as well assume the best.

What Doesn't Matter...

◎ Other people's negativity. It's up to you to set the tone in your relationships.

◎ Punishing others. That's not your job, and it's not your responsibility.

◎ Punishing yourself. That's not your job either. Take your failings to God.

◎ Feelings of inferiority. Your self-worth comes from God, and He cherishes you.

◎ Feelings of superiority. If your self-worth comes from God, it doesn't make you think less of other people.

Focus Points...

By the grace of God I am what I am, and his grace toward me has not been in vain.
1 CORINTHIANS 15:10 NRSV

Be of the same mind toward one another; do not be haughty in mind, but associate with the lowly. Do not be wise in your own estimation.
ROMANS 12:16 NASB

He replied, "My kindness is all you need. My power is strongest when you are weak." So if Christ keeps giving me his power, I will gladly brag about how weak I am.
2 CORINTHIANS 12:9 CEV

God has chosen you and made you his holy people. He loves you. So always do these things: Show mercy to others, be kind, humble, gentle, and patient.
COLOSSIANS 3:12 NCV

what really counts

Nothing whatever pertaining to godliness and real holiness can be accomplished without grace.

SAINT AUGUSTINE

Our worst days are never so bad that you are beyond the reach of God's grace. And your best days are never so good that you are beyond the need of God's grace.

JERRY BRIDGES

What Matters Most to Me About
Personal Growth

If you are in Christ, you have become righteous in God's sight. Now you're becoming what you have already become. You are being shaped into a person who looks more like Christ, as God finishes the work He began in you.

◎ *A solid and true life is lived from the inside out. What are the places in your life where the outside—the part of you that everyone else sees—doesn't match up with the inside? How can you bring the outside and the inside into alignment?*

_____

_____

_____

_____

_____

_____

_____

_____

◎ *Reflect on Philippians 4:8. What are some true, noble, reputable, authentic, and compelling things you can dwell on? Be specific.*

_____

_____

_____

_____

_____

_____

_____

_____

◎ *The meditation on desire began with two questions: What do you really want? And what need do you think would be fulfilled if you got what you wanted? Record your answers to those two questions. And while you're at it, reflect on how God can meet those needs.*

_____

_____

_____

_____

_____

_____

_____

_____

_____

◎ *Make a list of the people you're trying to please. Now think about the things you do to please them. Are any of those things out of line with what pleases God?*

_____

_____

_____

_____

_____

_____

_____

_____

_____

A saint is someone whose life makes
it easier to believe in God.
WILLIAM BARCLAY

HEAVEN

An Introduction

> You laid earth's foundations a long time ago, and handcrafted the very heavens.
>
> PSALM 102:25 MSG

what really counts

When people talk about heaven, do you have a hard time thinking of it as a real place? Pearly gates and streets of gold seem far, far away. You still have a lot of living you want to do. You want to finish school, start a career, and live on your own. Most likely, you have plenty of friends and family around to keep you company, so why even think about heaven? In fact, there are several paradise-like places on earth that you'd love to visit, ones that feature pearly-white-capped mountains and golden beaches.

But the reality is, your stay here on earth is just a short blip on the radar of time. Even if you live to be more than a hundred years old, that's still nothing compared to how long you'll exist eternally. As you get older, you'll become more personally aware of how much suffering goes on in this world. People you love will pass on, and you'll long to see them again in eternity. What can you do now while you're young?

For starters, spend some time in the Word reading about heaven. It's a real place where God makes His throne, surrounded by splendor. At His right hand sits Jesus, who is interceding for you every minute. One day you'll enter the enormous grandeur of God's creativity and love, and all your questions will be answered in an instant. Is there anybody you'd miss if you knew you'd never see them again? Now's the best time to give them a message of eternal hope.

Death … is no more than passing from one room into another. But there's a difference for me, you know. Because in that other room, I shall be able to see.

HELEN KELLER

Heaven
The Final Milestone

> Just as the heavens are higher than the earth, my thoughts and my ways are higher than yours.
>
> ISAIAH 55:9 CEV

what really counts

On the day you entered the world, everything you did was seen as an absolute miracle. You cried, and everybody clapped. Your mom scribbled your weight and length on pink or blue announcements and sent them out to everyone she knew. Every sprig of hair on your head was touched, and any achievement was recorded with joy. All you had to do was breathe or wiggle your toes and your family thought you were the greatest thing ever.

Then along came your other milestones: first word, first step, first day of school. One day, your baby book got stuffed under a bed, and now you're in charge of keeping up with your own accomplishments. You have your own set of goals now. If you're a good athlete, maybe you're aiming for a full college scholarship or going pro with your talents. If you have a creative bent, you might plan on making a CD or showcasing your artistic works in a solo exhibition. Financially, your dream might be to start your own business and support yourself.

But no matter what you think will make you complete, you'll find that it's never enough. Once you reach a milestone, you'll notice things are not quite perfect, and you want to go a little further. You get on the college team, but now you want to impress everybody by becoming the top scorer. You want your CD to go platinum or your artwork to sell to exclusive, high-end markets. When your business starts churning a profit, you decide it's time to upgrade and increase your income. A little ambition can be a good thing, but you'll wonder why you're never perfectly content.

Happiness and fulfillment always seem to be waiting at the next milestone. But one day you'll discover that heaven is the final milestone. There, in the presence of God, you will find the rest and fulfillment that you get only a foretaste of on earth. All of your accomplishments will pale in comparison to sitting in the presence of almighty God. He's expecting you. Jesus has gone ahead and prepared your room. He said, "I will come back and take you to be with me so that you may be where I am" (John 14:3 NCV). When you arrive, you'll finally be able to see your Maker face-to-face and thank Him for the good life He gave you.

Heaven
The Final Milestone

What Matters Most...

- ◉ Eternity. Don't get so caught up in your dreams and goals that you lose sight of where you're ultimately headed.

- ◉ God's Word. It's filled with truths that will make greater sense the more life experiences you go through.

- ◉ Faith. Hold on to it. One day, it will be all you have.

- ◉ Patience. Keep holding out for the final milestone that matters most.

- ◉ Trust. It's hard to believe in what you can't see, but Jesus is waiting for you in a real place.

What Doesn't Matter...

- ◉ Earthly treasures. They can rot, rust, or be stolen, so set your heart on treasures that last forever.

- ◉ Athletic, creative, or financial accomplishments. They won't help you earn your way into heaven.

- ◉ Lack of contentment. You can never expect to be perfectly fulfilled until you can finally rest in heaven.

- ◉ Self-actualization. Keep your focus on God, not on pop psychology that's based on human ideas.

- ◉ Knowing all the answers. The great news is, you don't have to understand everything right now.

Focus Points...

Thus says the LORD: "Heaven is My throne, and earth is My footstool."
ISAIAH 66:1 NKJV

Not everyone who calls me "Lord, Lord" will enter the Kingdom of heaven, but only those who do what my Father in heaven wants them to do.
MATTHEW 7:21 GNT

God has promised us a new heaven and a new earth, where justice will rule. We are really looking forward to that!
2 PETER 3:13 CEV

May you be blessed by the LORD, the Maker of heaven and earth.
PSALM 115:15 NIV

what really counts

This is what the Son promised to us—life forever.
1 JOHN 2:25 NCV

It is glorious to be far out on the ocean of divine love, believing in God, and steering for Heaven straight away by the direction of the Word of God.

CHARLES SPURGEON

One short sleep past, we wake eternally, and Death shall be no more; Death, thou shalt die.

JOHN DONNE

Heaven
The Real You

> Our citizenship is in heaven, from which we also eagerly wait for the Savior, the Lord Jesus Christ.
>
> PHILIPPIANS 3:20 NKJV

what really counts

If you've ever watched a house being built from scratch, you know it's a very involved and fascinating process. At first, you see only a hole in the ground, and a few people standing around with sheets of paper covered in line drawings. The site manager points here and there, and giant concrete trucks start dumping in tons of cement to pour a foundation. Then the framers come and start hammering and pounding in a wooden skeletal frame. You're trying to picture how it will look when it's finished, but it just looks like mud and boards to you.

In time, though, you get to see the finished product, covered in brick or siding, and the lit-up interior sparkles with glass and brass and tile. Oh, it finally makes sense now! When you go back and look at the architect's plans, you can envision exactly what he was thinking about.

Your life is similar to a house being built as you undergo the step-by-step process of becoming the man or woman God designed you to be. You're designed by God, the Head Architect, who has been perfecting His plans for you for a long time. But you can't see the completed building yet.

There's a real you that God can see, but while you're young, your construction site may seem unfinished and a little muddy. The real you looks a lot like Christ, as He builds you up layer by layer, conforming you more to His image. You'll be worked on daily until the minute you step into heaven. There you'll be perfected like Christ, for you will see Him as He is. Be careful that you don't let anything get in the way of His building process. Scripture says, "If the LORD doesn't build the house, the builders are working for nothing" (Psalm 127:1 NCV).

When you're young, you may not feel like you're becoming a spectacular custom-built estate, but God's Word says you are. Your foundation and capstone are Christ, and "you also, like living stones, are being built into a spiritual house to be a holy priesthood" (1 Peter 2:5 NIV). It can be hard to wait for that finished product, but when you get to heaven, everything will all come together. Hang in there, and keep your hopes on the Designer who's building you up to join Him forever.

Heaven
The Real You

What Matters Most...

◎ Trusting God. He knows what He has in mind for you.

◎ Being patient. You want to be solidly built, instead of like a shack that blows over in a day.

◎ Realizing that perfection will come. It may not seem possible, but the real you will be *perfect* one day.

◎ Putting your hope in the Head Architect. Don't let yourself get discouraged with the muddy process of character growth.

◎ Filling your rooms with wisdom. God's Word will make you wise and rich in truth.

What Doesn't Matter...

◎ The time it takes. Your whole life is a slow process toward perfection, but the timing is God's.

◎ The rainy days when no progress is made. You need days off to rest and refocus anyway.

◎ The fear you feel that you're not in control. You have a master Designer in charge of the process.

◎ Difficulties. Character growth is hard sometimes.

◎ Your frustration that the plans aren't visible to you. The more you treasure the Bible's wisdom, the more the plans will become clear.

Focus Points...

Now all we can see of God is like a cloudy picture in a mirror. Later we will see him face to face. We don't know everything, but then we will, just as God completely understands us.
1 CORINTHIANS 13:12 CEV

My own hand laid the foundations of the earth, and my right hand spread out the heavens.
ISAIAH 48:13 NIV

Every house has a builder, but the Builder behind them all is God.
HEBREWS 3:4 MSG

By the word of God heaven was made, and the earth was made from water and with water.
2 PETER 3:5 NCV

what really counts

Oh come, let us worship and bow down; let us kneel before the LORD our Maker.
PSALM 95:6 NKJV

The best we can hope for in this life is a knothole peek at the shining realities ahead. Yet a glimpse is enough.
JONI EARECKSON TADA

Aim at heaven and you will get earth thrown in. Aim at earth and you will get neither.
C. S. LEWIS

What Matters Most to Me About
Heaven

Although it may seem like the earth is your home, you're heading a little bit closer to your everlasting residence every day. What are your thoughts on heaven?

◎ *Isaiah 66:1 describes heaven as God's throne and earth as His footstool. Look all around you. Does that Scripture make you feel differently about your life on earth?*

_____

_____

_____

_____

_____

_____

_____

_____

◎ *What are some ideas you have about what life will be like in heaven? What are the main influences that helped shape your ideas?*

_____

_____

_____

_____

_____

_____

_____

_____

◎ *How does a person enter heaven? Do you feel confident that you will have an open invitation? Why or why not?*

_____

_____

_____

_____

_____

_____

_____

_____

_____

◎ *What is the first question you'd like to ask God when you enter heaven?*

_____

_____

_____

_____

_____

_____

_____

_____

_____

_____

How sweet is rest after fatigue! How sweet will heaven be when our journey is ended.

GEORGE WHITEFIELD

PRAYER

An Introduction

> When you pray, go into your room, and when you have shut your door, pray to your Father who is in the secret place; and your Father who sees in secret will reward you openly.
>
> MATTHEW 6:6 NKJV

what really counts

During your teenage years, you begin to feel this intense desire to separate your faith from that of your parents. You're not a kid anymore, believing what you've heard all your life; you have your own mind, and you want to think things through for yourself. Although you may still have to load up with your parents to go to church on Sunday, what goes on in your heart between you and God is all yours. That personal, dynamic relationship with God can't be seen or touched by anyone else, and it all comes as a result of prayer.

Your prayer life is like water. If you continually keep the communication lines open with God, your spiritual growth will be like a fresh-flowing stream, moving along quickly. But if you stop praying, that water will become stagnant, like a summertime puddle full of mosquitoes. It's up to you to keep the words flowing between your heart and God's.

When you look at the life of Jesus, you see that He was constantly in prayer. After a busy day of teaching and performing miracles, Scripture says He went off by Himself and spent time with His heavenly Father. You need alone time in prayer as well. Prayer keeps you open to God's views, and allows Him to change you to be more like Him. When you pray regularly, it will enable you to "be transformed by the renewing of your mind, that you may prove what is that good and acceptable and perfect will of God" (Romans 12:2 NKJV).

> To be a Christian without prayer is no more possible than to be alive without breathing.
> MARTIN LUTHER

Prayer
Thinking Godward

Never stop praying, especially for others. Always pray by the power of the Spirit. Stay alert and keep praying for God's people.

EPHESIANS 6:18 CEV

what really counts

Do you ever have an interesting experience, then immediately start thinking how you can shape it into a story to tell your friends or family? The words go around in your head until you have the exact details and punch line to hold your listeners captive. What about your audience of God? Do you get excited about sharing your life events with Him? It's a good habit to think about how every experience could be shaped into a prayer. It's about thinking Godward, relating every thought, every experience to God.

Step back in time a minute and imagine that you were a spectator at the ninth-century BC showdown of the gods on Mount Carmel. It was a scene that even Steven Spielberg would have loved to capture with special effects. If you need a refresher, you'll find a recap in 1 Kings 18. God's faithful prophet Elijah was about to experience his moment of glory. But wait a minute—this was not his grand moment; it was

God's. All day, the Baal worshipers had been dancing around their altar, screaming and slashing at themselves, trying to get their phony god to light it on fire. The echoing voices of the thousands must have been extraordinary.

Then it was finally Elijah's turn. "Pray louder!" he said to them. "If Baal really is a god, maybe he is thinking, or busy, or traveling! Maybe he is sleeping so you will have to wake him!" (1 Kings 18:27 NCV). At last, they gave up, so Elijah repaired the old, busted Israelite altar and surrounded it with a trench filled with water. And then he prayed, "Answer me, O LORD, answer me, so these people will know that you, O LORD, are God" (1 Kings 18:37 NIV). Within seconds, God sent blazing bolts of fire straight from heaven that burned up the sacrifice, the wood, the stones, the soil, even the water in the trench!

Think about those toasted ashes left there on Mount Carmel the next time you wonder if God is listening to your prayers. Elijah prayed, and God responded. If you keep reading, you'll find that Elijah didn't run around basking in his personal glory. He slipped away to a mountaintop to continue praying. His life serves as an example even now. Let God in on the events of your life, inviting Him into your glory and pain. You never have to feel alone.

Prayer
Thinking Godward

What Matters Most...

- Inviting God into your life. Let His Word dwell in you richly and in everything you say or do.

- Thinking Godward. When you experience something, turn your thoughts to letting God in on it.

- Focusing on Christ when you share with others. You can say, "Look what God is doing in my life!"

- Praying. Praying. Praying. At all times. Period.

- Seeing life as an adventure in how God will answer your prayers. Trust Him to lead you in making and following through with the right choices.

What Doesn't Matter...

- Immediate results. Unfortunately, prayers that result in thunderbolts from heaven are a pretty rare occurence.

- Friends and family who don't believe God is working. You can't win them over on your own.

- Personal failure. Someday, you'll see why you had to go through hardships that don't make any sense now.

- Lack of motivation. You may not feel like turning your thoughts Godward, but try to make it a lifetime habit.

- Bad days. Everybody has them. But there are plenty of good days as well.

Focus Points...

Even when you do pray, your prayers are not answered, because you pray just for selfish reasons.
JAMES 4:3 CEV

The prayer of a righteous man is powerful and effective.
JAMES 5:16 NIV

When my life was slipping away, I remembered GOD, and my prayer got through to you, made it all the way to your Holy Temple.
JONAH 2:7 MSG

It came to pass, as He was praying in a certain place, when He ceased, that one of His disciples said to Him, "Lord, teach us to pray, as John also taught his disciples."
LUKE 11:1 NKJV

what really counts

If you remain in me and follow my teachings, you can ask anything you want, and it will be given to you.
JOHN 15:7 NCV

We begin praying for others by first quieting our fleshly activity and listening to the silent thunder of the Lord of hosts.

RICHARD FOSTER

Anything big enough to occupy our minds is big enough to hang a prayer on.

GEORGE MACDONALD

Prayer
If You Only Knew

> The eyes of the LORD are on the righteous, and His ears are open to their prayers.
>
> 1 PETER 3:12 NKJV

what really counts

Do you ever feel something so strongly in your heart that you just know it's God's will? You might feel you're pleasing God just by praying for it. *It can't be long*, you think, *before this prayer is answered.* Instead, you sometimes have to go through the agony of realizing God has another plan for your life. Other times, you hear nothing, and you're forced to wait. And wait. And wait.

This happened to filmmaker Ken Wales. He had to wait nearly two decades to receive an answer to a prayer. In 1975, after reading Catherine Marshall's best-selling novel *Christy*, he felt that God was calling him to make it into a movie. But when he contacted the author, she told him the film rights had already been sold. And nothing was happening—no film was being made. Wales prayed for God's timing, and nineteen years later, he finally owned the rights and could begin filming his dream project.

To his amazement, he discovered that the lead actress, nineteen-year-old Kellie Martin, was born in the exact month he had begun feeling God's call to produce the story. "I had to wait for her to grow up to play Christy!" he said. Although Wales had originally hoped to make a feature-length movie, God opened doors for him to produce a television series instead. The first night it appeared on television, forty million viewers tuned in to watch the series on a major network. "As I see now in hindsight, God's timing is perfect," he said. "More people saw *Christy* on TV in one night than would have seen the feature film in a lifetime."

Despite hearing stories like this, it's still hard to wait for an answer to prayer. Maybe you're impatient to hear back concerning a college application. Or maybe you feel abandoned by someone you love deeply, and you long for God to bring that person back into your life. It may be years before you understand why God would allow you to go through the pain of being lonely. You can't see the whole big picture of your life the way God can. From your perspective, you see unanswered prayer. But only God knows how He's working in your life, preparing you to receive what's best, even if you've prayed for something else. "This hope will never disappoint us, because God has poured out his love to fill our hearts" (Romans 5:5 NCV).

Prayer
If You Only Knew

What Matters Most...

◎ Abiding in Christ. Prayer develops your relationship with Him.

◎ Remaining in the Word. Don't let a day go by without reading at least one verse.

◎ Reading stories of other people's prayers being answered. They'll give you hope in seeing how God works.

◎ Loving God for who He is. He's your Father who loves you 365 days a year.

◎ Remembering your experiences of prayer. Write them down, so you'll have a record of what happens.

What **Doesn't** Matter...

◎ Your frustration. Let God know you're struggling, and open yourself up to His ideas.

◎ Your timing. You think you know what's best for your life, but you can't see what God already knows.

◎ Your plans. Put them in God's hands and let Him be your dream manager.

◎ Your bargaining with God. Do you ever pray, "God, if You'll *only* do this, I'll . . ."? That's not submitting completely to His will.

◎ Your wanting to give up. Remain steadfast and put your hope in God's plan for your future.

Focus Points...

Be still, and know that I am God; I will be exalted among the nations, I will be exalted in the earth.
PSALM 46:10 NIV

I do not pray for these alone, but also for those who will believe in Me through their word.
JOHN 17:20 NKJV

Be cheerful no matter what; pray all the time; thank God no matter what happens. This is the way God wants you who belong to Christ Jesus to live.
1 THESSALONIANS 5:16–18 MSG

When He came to the place, He said to them, "Pray that you may not enter into temptation."
LUKE 22:40 NKJV

what really counts

Prayer is a matter of giving ourselves to God and learning His laws, so that He can do through us what He wants the most.

AGNES SANFORD

We forget that God sometimes has to say No. We pray to Him as our heavenly Father, and like wise human fathers, He often says, No, not from whim or caprice, but from wisdom and from love, and knowing what is best for us.

PETER MARSHALL

Prayer
Prayer Changes Things

> Delight yourself also in the LORD, and He shall give you the desires of your heart.
>
> PSALM 37:4 NKJV

what really counts

Prayer has been the backbone of many movements, and one of the most explosive results of prayer has been the growth of Christianity in Korea. In the past century, that nation has gone from having very few Christians to boasting nearly one-third of its population as followers of Christ. In fact, you'll find the largest Christian church in the world in Seoul, Korea. There, the Yoido Full Gospel Church has an incredible seven hundred thousand members! Since the church building can hold only twenty-five thousand attendees at once, the pastor offers seven services on Sunday, two on Saturday, and several more during the week. You may want to add this church to your list of amazing places you want to someday visit.

What happened in Korea came about as a result of years of fervent prayer, from missionaries and from the small community of Christian believers. While no one in the early years could envision such a huge church in the works, God revealed His plan according to His own timing. The prayers of the people affected the history of a whole nation, and the changes began individually, heart by heart, as new believers bowed down in prayer.

In the same way, God listens to your prayers as you focus your heart and mind on communicating with Him. It's a mystery how prayer works, because we know that God is sovereign over all creation; He already knows what's going to happen in the future. But who's to say that events don't come about because people sought Him out and prayed? When you bow to Him, you're following the example He gave as He walked the earth as the Son of God. What if you're not even sure what you want to say to God? He'll help you. Scripture says, "The Spirit helps us with our weakness. We do not know how to pray as we should. But the Spirit himself speaks to God for us, even begs God for us with deep feelings that words cannot explain" (Romans 8:26 NCV). It's nice to know that God is even helping you out with what to pray for. As you seek spending time with God through prayer, you'll begin to notice more and more changes taking place in your life. The real point of prayer is that it gives you a new way to see things—God's way. It's a lifetime process that only gets richer with each passing year.

Prayer
Prayer Changes Things

What Matters Most...

- Maintaining an active prayer life and leaving the long-time results to God.

- Memorizing Scriptures that encourage you to focus on truth.

- Studying the prayers of Jesus and other people in the Bible.

- Listening to God and trying to change to please Him.

- Praising Him through your words and through Scripture.

What **Doesn't** Matter...

- Worrying about words. The Holy Spirit intercedes for you, even if you can't think of the words to say.

- Having a beautiful, peaceful mountaintop for your prayer time. God can listen to you anywhere at any time.

- Understanding how prayer works. Accept that it's a mystery, and you'll be able to have your questions answered someday.

- Waiting until you feel spiritual. Feelings shouldn't get in the way of your faith.

- Comparing your prayers to other people's prayers and feeling like your prayers are kind of dorky. God loves your heart.

Focus Points...

Where two or three are gathered together in My name, I am there in the midst of them.
MATTHEW 18:20 NKJV

Look deep into my heart, God, and find out everything I am thinking. Don't let me follow evil ways, but lead me in the way that time has proven true.
PSALM 139:23–24 CEV

Ask, and it will be given to you; seek, and you will find; knock, and it will be opened to you.
MATTHEW 7:7 NKJV

Come near to God, and God will come near to you ... You who are trying to follow God and the world at the same time, make your thinking pure.
JAMES 4:8 NCV

what really counts

Christ's life outwardly was one of the most troubled lives that was ever lived: tempest and tumult, tumult and tempest, the waves breaking over it all the time. But the inner life was a sea of glass. The great calm was always there.

HENRY DRUMMOND

The one concern of the devil is to keep Christians from praying ... He laughs at our toil, mocks at our wisdom, but trembles when we pray.

SAMUEL CHADWICK

245

What Matters Most to Me About
Prayer

Prayer may seem completely natural to you. You can't imagine going a day without chatting with your heavenly Father. Or it could be a chore you've been avoiding. Write down some thoughts here.

◎ *Read the Lord's Prayer in Matthew 6:9–13. You've probably had it memorized for years, but is there anything you can apply to your own prayer life today?*

_____

_____

_____

_____

_____

_____

_____

_____

◎ *Why do you think Jesus often went alone to pray to God?*

_____

_____

_____

_____

_____

_____

_____

_____

what
really
counts

○ Have you received an answer to a prayer lately? Write down your experience here.

_____

_____

_____

_____

_____

_____

_____

_____

_____

○ Some people use the acronym ACTS when they pray: Adoration, Confession, Thanksgiving, and Supplication. Do you think these are good steps to prayer? Why or why not?

_____

_____

_____

_____

_____

_____

_____

_____

_____

_____

PRAYER

Is prayer your steering wheel or your spare tire?

CORRIE TEN BOOM

SIN

An Introduction

> Be strong and courageous; do not be afraid nor dismayed ... with us is the LORD our God, to help us and to fight our battles.
>
> 2 CHRONICLES 32:7–8 NKJV

what really counts

If you were on a cruise ship coasting through crystal-blue island waters right now, your thoughts would be completely relaxed. You might be basking in the warm sunshine beside the ship-deck pool or napping quietly under a brilliant, starry sky. Your cares and worries would be left behind; after all, this is your vacation. You certainly would not be on the lookout for enemies or danger.

But as you voyage through this once-only trip called life, you're not a passenger on a luxury ocean liner; you're a soldier on a battleship. The enemy is always around you, constantly lurking "like a roaring lion, seeking whom he may devour" (1 Peter 5:8 NKJV). He's looking for your weak points, so he can launch a missile at you. Soldiers on a battleship are not in a mode of leisure; they're ready to attack or to defend themselves at all times. They've had months or years of training and are prepared to use it.

Sure, soldiers have downtime to fellowship and relax, but they're constantly ready on a moment's notice to fight a battle. The Bible tells you to "put on God's full armor. Then on the day of evil you will be able to stand strong" (Ephesians 6:13 NCV). Although the devil can tempt and entice you to go astray, he has no power to force you to sin. Be ready for him, as a soldier is ready. Know the Word, and be prepared to stand firm in your faith.

> Where there is fear of God to keep the house, the enemy can find no way to enter.
> SAINT FRANCIS OF ASSISI

Sin

Repent: The Kingdom of God Is at Hand

> The Lord isn't slow about keeping his promises, as some people think he is. In fact, God is patient, because he wants everyone to turn from sin and no one to be lost.
>
> 2 PETER 3:9 CEV

what really counts

When you're out on the court or field competing in a sports event, you can hear the voices of spectators cheering you on from the stands. Your coach and fellow team members also shout out words of inspiration for you. But your opponent has his own cheering section as well. You try to block out the voices rooting for your rival and focus instead on the encouragement meant for you.

The same thing that happens in the sports arena takes place every day in your heart. There are two opposing sides in a constant battle, and you will turn toward one and turn away from the other. One voice wants you to please God; the other wants you to turn away. For example, a friend asks you to sneak the answers to a test you took the class period before her. You think, *It's okay. I'm helping her out, and someday she'll help me out.* Or it's Friday night, and you notice that it's ten minutes until your curfew. You know you should be getting home so your parents won't be worried, but you're having way too much fun talking to your friends. What should you do?

Listen to that still, small voice that pricks your conscience and reminds you who's in charge of your life. It's God, longing to communicate with you. He wants the best for you. When you ignore His voice and do something you later regret, your guilt will steal away any feelings of joy. In fact, your guilt may make it impossible for you to find fellowship with God. But your heavenly Father wants you to turn back to Him. That's what repentance means—a turning, a changing of the mind.

When police are searching for a criminal hiding in the dark, the first thing they do is expose the crime scene with bright light. The crook will either scurry away into the darkness or stand there frozen in the light's captivity. When you feel caught or trapped in your sin, you don't have to stand there handcuffed and hopeless. It's never too late to turn away from sin and turn toward God. You have assurance: "If we confess our sins, He is faithful and just to forgive us our sins and to cleanse us from all unrighteousness" (1 John 1:9 NKJV). Sin has consequences, but you can be forgiven. You can turn and move on with a heart that's clean and free.

Sin
Repent: The Kingdom of God Is at Hand

What Matters Most...

- Recognizing your sin for what it is. It is ugly, and it needs to be dealt with.

- Confessing your sin to God and asking for His forgiveness.

- Thanking God that the promises in His Word are true, and that He has cleansed your heart.

- Accepting His forgiveness and moving on with your life.

- Sharing with your friends and family how they, too, can live in fellowship with God.

What Doesn't Matter...

- How bad your sin is. God sees all sin as equal before His eyes, and He wants to forgive you.

- How much time has passed. It's never too late to seek out God's forgiveness.

- How hard it is to let go of feelings. Let God have your heart, and He'll fill it with truth.

- How many other people are involved. You're not responsible for their sins, only for your own.

- How you've lived in the past. God's ready to transform your life and make it fresh and new.

Focus Points...

Forget the former things; do not dwell on the past. See, I am doing a new thing! Now it springs up; do you not perceive it?
Isaiah 43:18–19 NIV

[John] said, "Turn back to God! The kingdom of heaven will soon be here."
Matthew 3:2 CEV

I say to you that likewise there will be more joy in heaven over one sinner who repents than over ninety-nine just persons who need no repentance.
Luke 15:7 NKJV

Direct my footsteps according to your word; let no sin rule over me.
Psalm 119:133 NIV

Distress that drives us to God ... turns us around. It gets us back in the way of salvation. We never regret that kind of pain.
2 Corinthians 7:10 MSG

what really counts

God has cast our confessed sins into the depths of the sea, and He's even put a "No Fishing" sign over the spot.

Dwight Moody

Either sin is with you, lying on your shoulders, or it is lying on Christ, the Lamb of God.

Martin Luther

Sin
Can You Pass This Test?

No temptation has overtaken you except what is common to humanity. God is faithful and He will not allow you to be tempted beyond what you are able.

1 CORINTHIANS 10:13 HCSB

what really counts

You're sitting in calculus class and you're supposed to be thinking about numbers, but your mind keeps wandering to the girl sitting across the room. You've known her since middle school, but suddenly you're noticing how she's grown up. You'd like to talk to her more, maybe take her to a movie. She's got this great smile and laugh. The only problem is, well, she's not a Christian. You've even heard her make fun of people who believe the Bible is true. But you wonder if maybe God wants to use you in her life. What's the big deal about dating someone who isn't a Christian?

While it's not a sin to go out with a person who doesn't share your faith, it does put you in a position of temptation. You may want to help her out, but she might end up dragging you down, causing you to compromise in areas where you now stand strong. Temptation itself isn't a sin; even Jesus faced temptation. Temptation is a test. And God always makes it possible for you to pass the test. He will not allow you to be tempted beyond what you can resist.

Think what Jesus went through when He was tempted by Satan in the desert. He had no food or water for forty days, and Satan knew He was thirsty and starving. He tempted Jesus to turn a stone to bread. Jesus responded immediately with Scripture: "It is written: 'Man does not live on bread alone'" (Luke 4:4 NIV). Notice that Jesus was armed with the Word as a weapon of attack. And Satan left Him alone.

How strong are you? For some people, it's better to just stay away from the battlefield altogether. Paul warned, "You are not the same as those who do not believe. So do not join yourselves to them" (2 Corinthians 6:14 NCV). If you do find yourself in tempting circumstances, be armed with Scripture. And be sure that nothing comes between you and your love for God. Sin has a way of creeping in and doing that. Be sure to "guard your heart, for it is the wellspring of life" (Proverbs 4:23 NIV). If you care about this girl, pray that God would bring Christian friends into her life. Let God work on her heart first, while you head back to your calculus.

Sin
Can You Pass This Test?

What Matters Most...

◎ Knowing Scripture. Hide it in your heart. Carry verses with you in your notebook to remind you of your priorities.

◎ Guarding your heart. Pray that God will keep your heart safe from sin.

◎ Being on the lookout for temptation. Don't get too complacent, or you'll find yourself not prepared for attack.

◎ Avoiding places and people that may cause you to stumble. Hang around people who are good influences on your life.

◎ Loving God more than anything or anyone else. It's the greatest commandment.

What **Doesn't** Matter...

◎ Feeling tempted. It's not a sin. Just don't let the temptation cause you to stumble.

◎ Feeling helpless against sin. Fight back with faith and Scripture. Surround yourself with wisdom from the Bible, godly people, and Christian books.

◎ Feeling like it's too late. Confess your mistake to God and get going again.

◎ Feeling alone in the battle. God promised in His Word that He would never leave you.

Focus Points...

Anyone who meets a testing challenge head-on and manages to stick it out is mighty fortunate. For such persons loyally in love with God, the reward is life and more life.
JAMES 1:12 MSG

I confessed my sins and told them all to you. I said, "I'll tell the LORD each one of my sins." Then you forgave me and took away my guilt.
PSALM 32:5 CEV

I beg you to avoid the evil things your bodies want to do that fight against your soul.
1 PETER 2:11 NCV

Therefore submit to God. Resist the devil and he will flee from you.
JAMES 4:7 NKJV

what really counts

Though we cannot eliminate temptation to sin, we are not left without redemptive resources. God is on our side, Jesus is advocating for us, and the Holy Spirit is making us aware of our weaknesses.

DAVID MCKENNA

The Christian life is not difficult; it is impossible. It is a supernatural life. When I try, I fail, but when I trust, God succeeds.

HOWARD HENDRICKS

What Matters Most to Me About
Sin

Scripture says, "All have sinned and are not good enough for God's glory" (Romans 3:23 NCV). But God wants you to confess your sins so He can forgive and cleanse you.

◉ *Name two or three areas in your life that you are struggling with now. Can you think of any specific changes you'd like to see take place in the next few months?*

_____

_____

_____

_____

_____

_____

_____

◉ *Write a prayer here, confessing these sins to God as He asks you to in 1 John 1:9.*

_____

_____

_____

_____

_____

_____

◉ *It helps to find someone who can listen to you as you work on these areas. What type of person do you think would make a good accountability partner? Do you know of anyone you'd like to ask for help?*

_____

_____

_____

_____

_____

_____

◉ *Before soldiers go off to fight, they're educated and trained to defeat their enemies. How about you? What are some ways you can prepare yourself to deal with difficult temptations you encounter every day at school or work?*

_____

_____

_____

_____

_____

_____

In the world it is called Tolerance, but in hell it is called Despair, the sin that believes in nothing, cares for nothing, seeks to know nothing, interferes with nothing, enjoys nothing, hates nothing, finds purpose in nothing, lives for nothing, and remains alive because there is nothing for which it will die.

DOROTHY SAYER

FAMILY AND RELATIONSHIPS
An Introduction

> In everything, therefore, treat people the same way you want them to treat you, for this is the Law and the Prophets.
>
> MATTHEW 7:12 NASB

what really counts

As Creator of the human family, God is intimately concerned with the role of family relationships. Throughout the Bible, many of His greatest works are accomplished through families. He even chose to come to earth as a Son who had earthly parents. Even from the cross Jesus looked after His mother's needs, asking the apostle John to take care of her. He places a high priority on how you treat your own mother and father, as well as your siblings and friends.

When you read through the Old Testament stories, one common feature is that many of God's people spent their entire lives traveling through deserts. There's a slim chance that you are sitting in a desert reading this book, but chances are you can look out the window right now and see at least one green thing growing. However, if you lived in a vast, arid wasteland with no permanent home and no way to start amassing a collection of stuff, your most important asset would be your relationships.

You wouldn't be known as the guy who had the coolest chariot in town or the girl with the biggest walk-in closet. You'd be so-and-so's daughter or son or cousin. Not that much has changed. Relationships with the people around you are still what really counts; they count more than anything you own. Jesus wants you to "love the Lord your God with all your heart and with all your soul and with all your mind" and to "love your neighbor as yourself" (Matthew 22:37–39 NIV).

> The way to love someone is to lightly run your finger over that person's soul until you find a crack, and then gently pour your love into that crack.
>
> KEITH MILLER

Family and Relationships

Honor Your Father and Your Mother

> My son, keep your father's commands and do not forsake your mother's teaching. Bind them upon your heart forever.
>
> PROVERBS 6:20–21 NIV

what really counts

It's Friday night, and you've worked all week so you can relax and chill over the weekend. You can't wait. First, you plan on taking in the early movie with some friends, then you'll have time to leisurely enjoy a double-cheese pizza and catch up with the group. But when you walk in the door from school, your mom reminds you that she needs your help tonight in taking a meal to your grandmother, who lives alone in a nursing home. You wonder if the time will ever come when you can make your own plans.

It can be tough when you're still living under your parents' roof, and you feel that they won't give you any freedom. You may feel like they just don't understand you. But this is the way it's always been. Nearly fifty years ago, your grandparents probably watched *Rebel Without a Cause*, starring the young, hip actor James Dean. In one scene, he shouts at his "old man," who doesn't understand him. He escapes the

262

house and angrily speeds away in his car. Your parents, even your grandparents, may have felt a similar rebellion toward their own parents as well.

When you feel as if your parents don't understand you, go to God and talk to Him. He's always ready to listen to you. As you outgrow your childhood and prepare for the emotional independence of adulthood, it can be a challenging transition. You want the freedoms you'll have when you're on your own, but it isn't time yet for you to handle the complete responsibilities. While you wait, Scripture tells you to honor your parents.

The best ways to show them respect are through the words you say to them and your actions. You may not always feel love, but it's best to respond in a way that would be pleasing to God. Imagine several glittery, golden apples resting on a silver platter. In Proverbs 25:11, this is the image the Bible gives of a word aptly spoken. When you speak words that show respect to your parents, God is always pleased. Honoring your parents is one of the Ten Commandments, the only one that promises you long life if you obey it. Even when your parents may have different ideas for how they want you to spend your weekend, honor your parents. Let God take care of your feelings.

Family and Relationships

Honor Your Father and Your Mother

What Matters Most...

◎ Honoring your parents through the way you talk to them and treat them.

◎ Obeying their rules as long as you live with them, even when you don't feel like they're being fair.

◎ Thanking them as often as you can for the good things they provide for you.

◎ Forgiving them for their faults. Your parents are only human and sometimes make mistakes.

◎ Sharing your life with them. They'd love to know what's important to you if you'd let them into your world.

What **Doesn't** Matter...

◎ Always knowing the best words to say. Sometimes a hug or a pat on the back goes further than words.

◎ Feeling like you can't live up to your parents' standards. Talk to them and find out what they really want from you.

◎ Dwelling on past mistakes and regrets. Don't let another day go by without trying to work things out.

◎ Watching your parents deal with their own struggles. They're responsible to God for their actions and attitudes.

Focus Points...

Honor your father and mother. Then you will live a long, full life in the land the LORD your God will give you.
EXODUS 20:12 NLT

If a man curses his father or mother, his lamp will be snuffed out in pitch darkness.
PROVERBS 20:20 NIV

Children, obey your parents because you are Christians. This is the right thing to do.
EPHESIANS 6:1 GOD'S WORD

Correct your children, and they will be wise; children out of control disgrace their mothers.
PROVERBS 29:15 CEV

what really counts

The basic source of conflict is ... power. It is defined as control—control of others, control of our circumstances, and especially control of ourselves.

JAMES DOBSON

When you know how much God is in love with you, then you can only live your life radiating that love. I always say love starts at home: family first and then your own town or city.

MOTHER TERESA

Family and Relationships
The Golden Rule

> Be kind and compassionate to one
> another, forgiving each other, just as
> in Christ God forgave you.
>
> EPHESIANS 4:32 NIV

You walk up to the counter in a department store, ready to check out. But instead of helping you, the salesclerk is busy smacking gum and talking on her cell phone. The seconds tick by, and she acts as if you don't even exist. You wonder what to do. Should you do something to get her attention, or should you keep waiting indefinitely?

When people ignore or treat you rudely, it's hard not to want to respond in the same way. It can be nearly impossible to keep yourself from saying things you later regret. It stems from the battle against your sin nature—sometimes you can overcome the urge, and other times you give in. The apostle Paul struggled with this and wrote, "I do not understand the things I do. I do not do what I want to do, and I do the things I hate" (Romans 7:15 NCV). How can you fight the urge to lash out with words that rip?

As a child, you probably heard the golden rule repeated hundreds of times—"Do to others what you want them to do to you" (Matthew 7:12 NCV). Although this command seems trite to hear, it's much harder to live out. What does it mean in real life? The old adage "Sticks and stones may break my bones, but words will never harm me" is actually not true at all, especially in your teen years. Cruel words can tear you apart as nothing else can.

In contrast, kind and loving words can build others up. You can make a person's day by seeking out a way to compliment him in a genuine way. The third chapter of James gives you a lesson in how to speak, reminding you that "the tongue also is a fire, a world of evil among the parts of the body" (3:6 NIV). Ouch! Do you have to be told your mouth is like fire? Yet you can learn to control it, through constantly asking the Holy Spirit to live and speak through you.

It's not easy, but you can learn to treat others the way you wish they would treat you. You'll end up being the kind of person others genuinely like to be around. Instead of telling off that gum-smacking clerk, search your brain and think of one nice thing to say to her—you just might make her day.

Family and Relationships
The Golden Rule

What Matters Most...

- ◎ Kindness. When you step beyond yourself to be kind to others, you'll develop a habit of treating people with respect.

- ◎ Forgiveness. Don't hold a grudge, even when you feel angry enough to spit fire. Learn when to let go and move on.

- ◎ Compassion. Put yourself in someone else's shoes. Imagine what he is going through, and try to genuinely care for his feelings.

- ◎ Self-control. It's impossible to tame your tongue without God's help, so ask Him to enable you.

- ◎ Love. Love is not a feeling; it is an action. Show it as often as you can.

What Doesn't Matter...

- ◎ Rude people. The world is full of them, but you don't have to join in and become one.

- ◎ Gossip. It can be irresistible to pass on those juicy bits of information, yet stop doing it by saying, "You know, I really don't think we should be talking about that."

- ◎ The crowd. You don't exist to please your peers; you were created in the image of God to please Him.

- ◎ Past experiences. Okay, you've blown it before, but every day is fresh and new, giving you another chance to try to live in a Christlike way.

Focus Points...

I'm telling you to love your enemies. Let them bring out the best in you, not the worst. When someone gives you a hard time, respond with the energies of prayer.
MATTHEW 5:44 MSG

Stop being angry and don't try to take revenge. I am the LORD, and I command you to love others as much as you love yourself.
LEVITICUS 19:18 CEV

We love because he first loved us.
1 JOHN 4:19 NRSV

You can have sincere love for each other as brothers and sisters because you were cleansed from your sins when you accepted the truth of the Good News. So see to it that you really do love each other intensely with all your hearts.
1 PETER 1:22 NLT

what really counts

The person who has a good friend and is a good friend is a very rich and fulfilled person indeed.

ADRIAN ROGERS

Friendship can be a mirror in which I am able to see myself and realize, by focusing on my friend, what I need to do to become more fully human.

MADELINE L'ENGLE

What Matters Most to Me About
Family and Relationships

As you practice ways of showing honor to your parents and love to others, you'll grow closer to God in your spiritual walk. Keep in contact with Him every day, through His Word and prayer.

◎ *How do you feel about your relationship with your parents? Are there any areas that you'd like to work on to improve things?*

_____

_____

_____

_____

_____

_____

_____

_____

◎ *Write down three ways you can show respect for your parents this week.*

_____

_____

_____

_____

_____

_____

_____

◎ *Give one example of how you've experienced the golden rule in your life lately. How did you feel about it?*

_____

_____

_____

_____

_____

_____

_____

_____

◎ *Read 1 John 4:19–21. Why do you love others? Write down a prayer to ask God to help you deepen your love for the people all around you.*

_____

_____

_____

_____

_____

_____

_____

_____

> Dare to love and to be a real friend. The love you give and receive is a reality that will lead you closer and closer to God as well as those whom God has given you to love.
>
> HENRI J. M. NOUWEN

SIGNIFICANCE

An Introduction

> Think how much the Father loves us. He loves us so much that he lets us be called his children, as we truly are.
>
> 1 JOHN 3:1 CEV

what really counts

Who are you? Why are you here on earth? What is the significance of your life? These all are questions worth pondering while you're still young. And everybody seems to have a different opinion. You can encounter thousands of books and speakers who approach the topic of significance from various angles. When you browse through the self-help section of any bookstore, you can see how many voices are vying for your attention.

But if you try to search for answers from sources apart from the Word of God, you'll end up totally confused. Many ask you to look "deep within" to find your self-worth. You can have great self-esteem, they say, by thinking only positively, letting go of the past, and reaching for the stars. But what happens when you look inside the heart of a person? According to the Bible, "the heart is deceitful above all things and beyond cure. Who can understand it?" (Jeremiah 17:9 NIV). You can't find your answers in your heart because it can't be trusted.

Instead, as a believer in Christ, your significance comes from the relationship you have with your Father in heaven. You're a child of the King of kings! It doesn't matter what you look like, say, or do—you'll always be worthy of every good thing bestowed upon the child of royalty. Stay clear of sources that teach you falsely. Spend your time loving this great Father of yours and seeing what He wants His child to do.

There's some task which the God of all the universe . . . has for you to do, and which will remain undone and incomplete until by faith and obedience you step into the will of God.

ALAN REDPATH

Significance
Mundane Spirituality

> Sometimes our humble hearts can help us more than our proud minds.
>
> 1 CORINTHIANS 8:2 MSG

what really counts

It's almost 4:00 p.m., and you long to do something fun and exciting after taking classes all day. Instead, you drive straight from school to your mundane job at the grocery store, putting food in plastic bags for people. You have the 4:00–10:00 p.m. shift, and then you have to write an essay for English class tomorrow. *Yawn.* You try to focus on what's good—you putting in six hours of work that will help pay your car insurance. But still, you wish you could do something that really mattered for a change.

It's easy to get caught up in thinking that your blah life at times is not important to God. You may count the minutes until the end of the school day, then look at your watch at least fifty times the next several hours you spend at work or doing other activities. You might be wondering when your real life can begin. One of the greatest Christian thinkers of all time, Oswald Chambers, said this: "It is in our place of humiliation that we find our true worth to God—that is where our faithfulness is revealed."

God's not as concerned with whether you're doing grand and exciting things; He's more interested in your character growth. You may be thinking you'll be worth more to Him if you're a straight-A student or you win awards at school or at work. But He's really watching you to see that you're becoming more like Him. As you study Christ, you'll see the beauty of His servanthood, His faith, His passionate prayer life. He wasn't too busy hanging out with the bigwigs to let little children sit on His lap and listen to Him tell stories.

What about that supermarket job? Everything you do has spiritual significance; you don't have a secular life that's separate from your spiritual life. Are you helping to build God's kingdom in your everyday life? When you're filling up those plastic bags, look in the eyes of your customers. Do you see an elderly man buying some medications and vitamins? Maybe he's worried about the news at his last doctor's visit. Or how about the tired-looking mom with more kids than groceries in her cart—you might be the only grown-up she's talked to all day. Go ahead; say something friendly and think of it as an act of spiritual service. God will be pleased.

Significance
Mundane Spirituality

What Matters Most...

◎ Humility. God wants you to take on the heart of a servant and put others before yourself.

◎ Service. Small acts of kindness build your character, and others may ask you what your motivation is—which will give you an opportunity to share your faith.

◎ Love. This is what it all boils down to—loving God and loving others more than yourself.

◎ Obedience. Even when you want to give up, keep going. Keep trying to please God.

◎ Faithfulness. Being on time for work, doing the best job you can, and not complaining are all ways to bring God glory.

What **Doesn't** Matter...

◎ Self-importance. It doesn't matter how menial the task—just do it the best way you know how.

◎ Achievements. God is looking at your heart and your character growth more than your earthly attainments.

◎ Excitement. Not every day can be a mountaintop experience; in fact, most of life is spent doing chores in the valley.

◎ Secular versus spiritual. There's no separation; you have one life, and everything you do either brings honor or dishonor to Christ.

Focus Points...

In all the work you are doing, work the best you can. Work as if you were doing it for the Lord, not for people.
COLOSSIANS 3:23 NCV

Let heaven fill your thoughts. Do not think only about things down here on earth.
COLOSSIANS 3:2 NLT

Act like people with good sense and not like fools.
EPHESIANS 5:15 CEV

I can do all things through Christ who strengthens me.
PHILIPPIANS 4:13 NKJV

This purity of faith is worth more than gold, which can be proved to be pure by fire but will ruin. But the purity of your faith will bring you praise and glory and honor when Jesus Christ is shown to you.
1 PETER 1:7 NCV

what really counts

We are not made for the mountains, for sunrises, or for the other beautiful attractions of life—those are simply intended to be moments of inspiration. We are made for the valley and for the ordinary things.

OSWALD CHAMBERS

If Christ does not reign over the mundane events in our lives, He does not reign at all.

PAUL TRIPP

Significance
Look Out, Look Up

> I press toward the goal for the prize of the upward call of God in Christ Jesus.
>
> PHILIPPIANS 3:14 NKJV

what really counts

Look around at your classmates, and you've probably got them pegged with a label in your mind. There are the athletes who seem to eat, drink, and sleep sports; the smart, nerdy ones who can take a computer apart and redesign it blindfolded; and the rah-rah fashion guys and girls who spend more time looking in the mirror than anything else. If you're the kind of person who's quick to judge others, that also means you're quick to judge yourself. And if you're looking at a person's worth from his or her outer looks or accomplishments, you probably seek your own self-worth in the same way.

It's hard not to value outside attractiveness and worldly success. You look up to people who set lofty goals and achieve them, so you expect the same for yourself. If you had to give yourself a label, what would it be? If God keeps a list of high achievers, you might be surprised to see who's on it. He's got

His eyes on what you can't see—the hearts of people. And He can also see down the long road ahead. Those peers of yours who focus on themselves and think only inwardly may not have the strength of character to survive when the first wave of disappointment crashes over them.

When you're looking for significance in your life, look outside yourself. Look up to God. Look out at the world around you. You were made for more than yourself. It doesn't seem that way—everywhere you look, people want you to get to know yourself better. You might enjoy taking those silly quizzes in magazines that get you to analyze who you are and what you're interested in. They're fun to browse through, but don't obsess about yourself too much.

Find things you can do to help others, especially people you know who might need some encouragement. What would Jesus say and do if He were at your school? He'd seek out the girl who eats lunch by herself because she's self-conscious about food getting stuck in her braces. Or the guy who stutters and is petrified of having to give reports in front of the class. When you stop focusing so much on who you are and what you want out of life, you'll see there are a lot of ways you can serve and love others.

Significance
Look Out, Look Up

What Matters Most...

◎ Looking upward to God. Praise and honor Him, not yourself.

◎ Looking outward at the world around you. Hey, there are a lot of exciting things going on outside your tiny corner of the earth.

◎ Looking for ways to help others. You have so much to offer; take the time to find ways.

◎ Looking for answers from God's Word. It will make you a wise person.

◎ Looking for success in God's eyes. He's your ultimate, lifelong Boss.

What Doesn't Matter...

◎ Labels. They just don't matter. You'll be surprised twenty years from now how people have changed when they show up at your class reunion.

◎ Outside appearances. God doesn't care how people look on the outside; it's their character that matters most.

◎ Giving excessive importance to academic/athletic/professional achievements.

◎ Others' opinions of you. Only God matters. Are you living your life to please Him?

◎ Self-actualization. Too much self-focus can drain your time and energy from serving others.

Focus Points...

Whoever desires to save his life will lose it, but whoever loses his life for My sake will find it.
MATTHEW 16:25 NKJV

Be devoted to one another in brotherly love. Honor one another above yourselves.
ROMANS 12:10 NIV

I, therefore, the prisoner of the Lord, beseech you to walk worthy of the calling with which you were called.
EPHESIANS 4:1 NKJV

Take away my foolish desires, and let me find life by walking with you.
PSALM 119:37 CEV

In Him dwells all the fullness of the Godhead bodily; and you are complete in Him, who is the head of all principality and power.
COLOSSIANS 2:9–10 NKJV

what really counts

A Christian should always remember that the value of his good works is not based on their number and excellence, but on the love of God which prompts him to do these things.

SAINT JOHN OF THE CROSS

An accurate understanding of God's truth is the first step toward discovering our significance and worth.

ROBERT S. MCGEE

What Matters Most to Me About
Significance

Does it really matter how you see yourself, or does it only matter how God sees you? It's best to take a balanced approach and consider both. Treat yourself the same way God treats you.

◎ *Who are some people you respect and look up to? What is it about these people that you value?*

_____

_____

_____

_____

_____

_____

_____

_____

◎ *Where do you find your self-worth? Do you find significance in your outside appearance or success? What do you think God values most about you?*

_____

_____

_____

_____

_____

_____

_____

what
really
counts

◎ *How does it change your view of yourself if you realize you are a child of God? What kinds of blessings are bestowed upon children of royalty?*

_____

_____

_____

_____

_____

_____

_____

_____

◎ *Write down some things you can do this week to show others you value them more than yourself.*

_____

_____

_____

_____

_____

_____

_____

_____

_____

Resolution One: I will live for God. Resolution Two: If no one else does, I still will.
JONATHAN EDWARDS

WORK

An Introduction

> We are His workmanship, created in Christ Jesus for good works, which God prepared beforehand that we should walk in them.
>
> EPHESIANS 2:10 NKJV

what really counts

When Saturday morning rolls around, it would take a bulldozer to get most students out of bed early. There's no ringing alarm clock, no honking bus or car ride, and no teacher waiting to write you up for being late. It feels great to lie back and ponder deep thoughts before you actually have to get up. But when it's Monday, there's no time for being lazy. When you're a student, school is work, and work is school.

You listen, write, and take tests all day. Then, as soon as the afternoon bell rings, you're most likely off to participate in sports, meetings, or part-time jobs— and these are your work as well. When you get home, you have homework, e-mail, and phone calls to keep you busy. And in the back of your mind, you're wondering what in the world you're going to choose for a career so you can live on your own someday.

Despite the great unknowns in your future, you do know one thing: God designed your body and mind for work. While you're in school, there's no better time to test your abilities and explore your interests. God loves the creative worker. You're surrounded by His workmanship—look at yourself, look all around you. "The heavens declare the glory of God; the skies proclaim the work of his hands" (Psalm 19:1 NIV). When you can focus your energies toward a singular purpose, your work can be fulfilling, or at least an act of obedience that brings glory to God.

> It is not what a man does that determines whether his work is sacred or secular, but why he does it.
>
> A. W. TOZER

Work
Whom Do You Work For?

Whatever you do, do your work heartily, as for the Lord rather than for men.

COLOSSIANS 3:23 NASB

what really counts

Do you remember your first job? Maybe your parents gave you a few dollars to rake leaves or wash the car. Or perhaps you earned a small fortune babysitting when you were in junior high. These early jobs may not have been glamorous, but they began developing your character and sense of financial responsibility. As a student, your main job is school, of course. Although it may seem like drudgery at times to keep on taking classes when you could be out in the "real world" earning some money, you'll go a lot farther in life if you hang in there and complete the highest degree you can at this point.

Although you don't get any payment for it, studying can be extremely hard work. When you're writing a paper or cramming for a test, it can be tempting to take as many short-cuts as possible. After all, you have a social life, part-time jobs, and other activities that consume your time as well. You may figure your teacher won't find out if you cut and paste straight from the Internet, or you "borrow" your friend's old project to present to the class. And it's true—your teachers are busy, and they may not have time to check out every Web site to see if you have plagiarized anything. But you're not working for them—you're working for God.

When you swallow that perspective, it changes the way you feel about cheating. There's nothing you can do that isn't seen and known by your heavenly Father—so He can't be fooled. It may seem like no big deal to swipe a few pens from the office where you work or to exaggerate your hours on your time sheet. But it's not your human bosses' opinions that really matter; it's your lifelong Boss who's always watching the way you live and work.

Instead of doing the least you possibly can to get by, try to follow these words of Jesus: "If someone forces you to go with him one mile, go with him two miles" (Matthew 5:41 NCV). You can probably name at least one person who lives this way. Maybe there's a person at your job who's always willing to switch with you if you need the day off. Think of ways you can walk the second mile in the classroom, at home, and at your job. When you work to please God, your teachers and human bosses may be pleasantly surprised.

Work
Whom Do You Work For?

What Matters Most...

◉ Working to please God. He is the only Boss who really matters, and He is always watching you.

◉ Being honest in all your endeavors. Even when you feel nobody will notice, keep doing what's right.

◉ Walking the extra mile. You'll be known as a person who can be depended upon.

◉ Avoiding the temptation to take the easy way out. Think ahead to what kind of person you want to be.

◉ Listening to your conscience. When your actions please God, you'll feel deep peace.

What **Doesn't** Matter...

◉ Short-term gain. What really counts is keeping your eyes on the long-term perspective.

◉ Admiration of others. Keep your focus on doing what's right and pleasing to God.

◉ Getting the highest grades at any cost. Just do the best you can, honestly.

◉ Pleasing only your teachers and earthly bosses. They are not your ultimate authority; God is.

◉ Making a ton of money. It's best to be honest and to do what God calls you to do.

Focus Points...

My dear friends, you always obeyed when I was with you. Now that I am away, you should obey even more. So work with fear and trembling to discover what it really means to be saved.
PHILIPPIANS 2:12 CEV

Don't work for food that spoils. Instead, work for the food that lasts into eternal life. This is the food the Son of Man will give you.
JOHN 6:27 GOD'S WORD

If anyone will not work, neither shall he eat.
2 THESSALONIANS 3:10 NKJV

Make it your goal to live quietly, do your work, and earn your own living, as we ordered you.
1 THESSALONIANS 4:11 GOD'S WORD

what really counts

Jesus said, "The food that keeps me going is that I do the will of the One who sent me, finishing the work he started."
JOHN 4:34 MSG

Make it your goal to be the best you can be at whatever task is set before you because it's your God-given work.
JERRY B. JENKINS

If a man does only what is required of him, he is a slave. If a man does more than is required of him, he is a free man.
CHINESE PROVERB

Work
Finding Your Calling

May the favor of the Lord our God rest upon us; establish the work of our hands for us—yes, establish the work of our hands.

PSALM 90:17 NIV

what really counts

People enjoy asking children the question "What do you want to be when you grow up?" If you were a kid who dug in the dirt with toy bulldozers, you probably told your parents, "I want to be a builder someday," and they smiled at you with those knowing looks of satisfaction. Or maybe you used to love putting bandages on your dolls, and you always thought you'd grow up to be a doctor or a vet. Ooh, but then things got complicated when you were completely grossed out dissecting the squishy parts of that pig in biology class. Now you feel more confused than ever.

You may feel like the pressure is on you right now to know exactly what you want to do with the rest of your life. You might be bombarded with filling out college applications, forcing you to write long-winded essays about your fabulous lifelong dreams and goals. And it's true—if you can convince an admissions officer that you have some pretty lofty visions for your future, you might get into your first-choice college and earn a great scholarship. But deep down you may be thinking, *I don't know! I just don't know!*

If you already know what you want to "be when you grow up," that's great. But if you don't, relax. No matter what field you major in, you're most likely going to change careers or jobs at least six or seven times anyway. It's really not all that important. In today's market, skill needs change quickly, and it's often your attitude and willingness to learn that matter more than anything. Rebecca St. James wrote, "I think as teenagers we need to be using these years to do God's will and make a difference. We are part of a generation He is calling to be sold out for Him."

Are you sold out for God? He's got your dream job under His control, and right now, He wants you to be preparing to be His worthy servant. You might become a prestigious architect someday, but what God wants for you is to be a man or woman who loves His Word. Or you might kick your squeamishness and become a world-renowned doctor. No matter what you do, live a life that makes an impact for God's kingdom; it's what really counts in the grand scheme of things.

Work
Finding Your Calling

What Matters Most...

◎ Prayer. Talk to God about your dreams and hopes for your future vocation.

◎ God's Word. Fuel up on truth every day, and God's plan for you will be slowly revealed.

◎ Focus. Don't get sidetracked on what really counts for your life.

◎ Long-term vision. Look at your heart and your character to define the kind of person you want to be someday.

◎ Patience. Just as a caterpillar has to stay crammed into a cocoon for a few weeks, you're developing slowly into a wonderful creation.

What Doesn't Matter...

◎ Knowing exactly what you want to do for the rest of your life—right this minute.

◎ Changing your career path as you grow older in order to develop your talents and interests.

◎ Exuding confidence at all times. It's okay to admit that you're not quite sure which direction you're headed.

◎ Being the perfect student who makes the perfect grades and has the perfect long-term plan. You're putting too much pressure on yourself.

◎ Choosing the career that everybody expects for you—you may want to blaze a new trail.

Focus Points...

I am confident of this very thing, that He who began a good work in you will perfect it until the day of Christ Jesus.
PHILIPPIANS 1:6 NASB

One who is slack in his work is brother to one who destroys.
PROVERBS 18:9 NIV

I keep trying to reach the goal and get the prize for which God called me through Christ to the life above.
PHILIPPIANS 3:14 NCV

In the same way, let your light shine before others, so that they may see your good works and give glory to your Father in heaven.
MATTHEW 5:16 NRSV

God is always at work in you to make you willing and able to obey his own purpose.
PHILIPPIANS 2:13 GNT

what really counts

Work is not primarily a thing one does to live, but the thing one lives to do. It is, or should be, the full expression of the worker's faculties, the thing in which he finds spiritual, mental, and bodily satisfaction.

DOROTHY SAYERS

When we are engaged in His work we are very close to Christ. We are expending our anxiety and affections on the same objects on which His heart is set.

JAMES STALKER

What Matters Most to Me About
Work

God already knows what His long-term vocation is for you, so it's most important that you hang out with Him in His Word. Take a few minutes to jot down some of your ideas about work.

◎ *What was your first job? Did you like it? Have you done any work that you really enjoyed doing, even if it was not for pay?*

_____

_____

_____

_____

_____

_____

_____

◎ *Do you have any idea what you would like to be doing in the future? Write down a list of your three top choices for careers. Is there a certain person whom you look up to who's doing one of these jobs?*

_____

_____

_____

_____

_____

_____

_____

◎ *What do you think most people find fulfilling about their work? Does this affect your choice of a long-term career goal?*

_____

_____

_____

_____

_____

_____

_____

_____

◎ *Think about what Rebecca St. James said about teens being "sold out" for God. How do you want your generation to make a difference in your world? What can you do personally to help fulfill this mission?*

_____

_____

_____

_____

_____

_____

_____

_____

_____

We ought not to be weary of doing little things for the love of God, who regards not the greatness of the work, but the love with which it is performed.

BROTHER LAWRENCE

MONEY

An Introduction

> It's obvious, isn't it? The place where your treasure is, is the place you will most want to be, and end up being.
>
> MATTHEW 6:21 MSG

what really counts

There are some topics that you won't find mentioned explicitly in the Bible, but money is not one of them. Although dollars and cents weren't around when it was written, Scripture has plenty to say about the unending struggle to master or be mastered by the acquisition of cold, hard cash. Face it: You have to have money to live, of course. Most likely, your parents work to put a roof over your head, food on your table, and clothes on your back. You aren't hurting for the bare necessities.

But come on! That's not all you need for survival, right? You have to have music, high fashion, concert and movie tickets, a car, and all the stuff you can't live without. What's the big deal about buying everything you want, especially if you work and buy it yourself?

It's a heart thing. There's nothing wrong with having money, but Jesus warned us, "Be careful and guard against all kinds of greed. Life is not measured by how much one owns" (Luke 12:15 NCV). It's so easy to get caught up in acquiring things you love and forget who gave them to you. Jesus wants to be sure your heart belongs to Him, not to the irresistible duds or DVDs you want to bring home. Sometimes it takes a trip to the children's hospital ward or to a third-world country to remind you that true wealth comes from valuing your walk with God and the hearts of people above all else.

> All that we have—our food, clothes, mind, energy, computer, money—everything we call ours comes from God . . . We will have to give Him a report on what we did with all His stuff.
> JOYCE MIRIAM BROOKS

Money
The Root of All Sorts of Evil

> Whoever loves money never has money enough; whoever loves wealth is never satisfied with his income. This too is meaningless.
>
> ECCLESIASTES 5:10 NIV

It's a story that's mentioned by three of the four Gospel writers, and it's been passionately discussed and debated for centuries. A wealthy young man came to see Jesus. No one knows what he looked like, but he was most likely dressed in the latest finery and may have been accompanied by servants. He was a good man who worked hard to do everything right, and he wanted to check salvation off his to-do list. He asked this great Teacher who seemed to know all the answers, "What good thing must I do to have life forever?" (Matthew 19:16 NCV).

Jesus saw straight through to the man's heart and was filled with compassion for him. He told him to obey the commandments, and named six of them specifically that concerned his relationship with others. No problem, the young man replied. He'd done these things all his life, so it looked like he was safe. Then Jesus went a step further; "There is one more thing you need to do. Go and sell everything you have, and give the money to the poor, and you will have treasure in heaven. Then come and follow me" (Mark 10:21 NCV).

The guy became very sad when he heard this—that would mean giving up all his wealth, and he just couldn't do it. Jesus knew the man was disobeying the first and most important commandment, found in Exodus 20:3, that he should have no other gods before his heavenly Father. Deep down, this man valued his possessions more than his relationship with God.

Does this story mean that Jesus wants you to give up everything you own to follow Him? Perhaps, if you love your stuff more than you love Him. When your passion for money overwhelms your passion for God's Word, then it's time to do a reality check and see if you have your heart in the right place. But you can look throughout the book of Proverbs and see that there's nothing intrinsically wrong with having an abundance. Many of God's chosen people were blessed with great wealth, and many of His followers today live quite well. You can still be a servant of God and live with your creature comforts if you are careful to "guard your heart, for it is the wellspring of life" (Proverbs 4:23 NIV). Honor God with your life by putting Him first, above all else.

Money
The Root of All Sorts of Evil

What Matters Most...

◎ Your heart. God wants to know that your relationship with Him is more important than anything you possess.

◎ Your stewardship. You need to take care of the income He gives you by giving back to Him and using your money wisely.

◎ Your values. By seeking first His kingdom (Matthew 6:33), you'll have your priorities in the right place when it comes to giving, saving, and spending.

◎ Your true love. Make sure it's God and not those crisp green bills.

◎ Your obedience. You need to be willing to obey God's commands about money.

What Doesn't Matter...

◎ How much money you have. If you're rich toward God and not things, that's what really counts.

◎ How much money someone else makes. Don't get caught in the trap of judging others or comparing yourself to them.

◎ How much stuff you own. It all belongs to God anyway.

◎ How you feel about being a good steward. It's an act of obedience, even when you feel that you can't possibly share anything.

Focus Points...

No one can serve two masters. He will hate the first master and love the second, or he will be devoted to the first and despise the second. You cannot serve God and wealth.
MATTHEW 6:24 GOD'S WORD

The more easily you get your wealth, the sooner you will lose it. The harder it is to earn, the more you will have.
PROVERBS 13:11 GNT

Certainly, the love of money is the root of all kinds of evil. Some people who have set their hearts on getting rich have wandered away from the Christian faith and have caused themselves a lot of grief.
1 TIMOTHY 6:10 GOD'S WORD

Don't be obsessed with getting more material things. Be relaxed with what you have ... God assured us, "I'll never let you down, never walk off and leave you."
HEBREWS 13:5 MSG

what really counts

God doesn't care about the size of your savings account, but He is interested in how much good you do with what you have.

MARTHA BOLTON

You say, "If I had a little more, I should be very satisfied." You make a mistake. If you are not content with what you have, you would not be satisfied if it were doubled.
CHARLES HADDON SPURGEON

Money
Your Money?

> Every generous act of giving, with every perfect gift, is from above, coming down from the Father of lights, with whom there is no variation or shadow due to change.
>
> JAMES 1:17 NRSV

what really counts

You have been given many things in this life. The very fact that you can read these words means you have been given the gift of eyesight as well as the gift of an education. If you had been born in a different part of the world, you might not have survived your infancy, much less attained a quality education. When you begin to realize that God is the source of everything you've received in this life, it makes you more aware of your great responsibility to be a good steward.

What is a *steward*? The word means "manager," one who takes care of things that don't belong to him. A steward who oversees a large estate or who works on a ship doesn't actually own this property. His job is to make sure the estate or boat is taken care of properly. You are the steward of many things. You've been given the resources of your time, your talents, and your treasures. Learning how to manage each of these gifts in the best way possible is a lifelong testing of your faith.

As a student, you may be thinking, *Hey, I'm barely getting by right now—don't even talk to me about managing money!* If you're in college, you may be floating on loans that you'll have to pay back, and the thought makes you want to hold on to every penny. But when you see the money you have as belonging to God, you'll be more careful to watch what becomes of it. There are ways for you to stretch your dollars and invest what you have wisely. As a steward managing what is God's property, you'll want to give what you can to help further His kingdom.

You can find dozens of Proverbs about the wise and foolish when it comes to money. How do you want to be regarded? There are times when you may come into a good bit of money, such as when you receive financial gifts for graduation. You can blow it away on little things, or you can pray about what God would have you do. You all know those adults who never seem to cease worrying about money; then there are those who feel peace about their finances. Your future very much depends on your stewardship skills that are in the process of being developed right now—so ask God to show you what to do with each dollar He gives you.

Money
Your Money?

What Matters Most...

- Asking God to show you how to be a good steward of the resources He has given you.

- Helping others when they are in need.

- Giving God back His share of what He has given you; for Christians this means to tithe regularly.

- Sharing your abundance with others.

- Being wise and careful in your stewardship and avoiding foolishness. A good way to do this is to read a chapter of Proverbs every day.

What Doesn't Matter...

- How much or how little you've been given. Do the best you can with what God has entrusted you.

- Comparing what others give to what you're able to give.

- Hoarding what little you have. Trust God that He will provide abundantly for your needs.

- Worrying about your future. Remain in God's Word, and He'll give you peace about your financial situation.

- Focusing on what you wish you had, instead of being grateful for what you're already blessed with.

Focus Points...

God has given a lot of faith to the poor people in this world. He has also promised them a share in his kingdom that he will give to everyone who loves him.
JAMES 2:5 CEV

Bring the full amount of your tithes to the Temple, so that there will be plenty of food there. Put me to the test and you will see that I will open the windows of heaven and pour out on you in abundance all kinds of good things.
MALACHI 3:10 GNT

Seek first his kingdom and his righteousness, and all these things will be given to you as well.
MATTHEW 6:33 NIV

A good man out of the good treasure of his heart brings forth good things, and an evil man out of the evil treasure brings forth evil things.
MATTHEW 12:35 NKJV

what
really
counts

The spirit of greed does not go away meekly. It keeps coming back. You have to deal with it, or it will win you.
RICHARD FOSTER

It isn't what we keep that counts, it's what we give. It's not what we hide away that counts; it's what we use.
OSWALD HOFFMAN

What Matters Most to Me About
Money

When you develop the perspective that you don't actually own your money, it changes what you want to do with it. Write down a few of your thoughts on what being a good steward means to you as a student.

◎ *How do you feel about your financial situation right now? Do you think you're living in abundance, or do you feel like you're barely getting by?*

_____

_____

_____

_____

_____

_____

_____

_____

◎ *Do you have a budget? Try to make a simple budget this week to keep track of your allowance or earnings and see where each dime is spent.*

_____

_____

_____

_____

_____

_____

_____

_____

what
really
counts

◎ *What are your long-term financial goals for the future? What would you like to be doing ten years from now? Twenty years from now?*

_____

_____

_____

_____

_____

_____

_____

_____

◎ *What steps can you take today to help you achieve those goals? Do you think they are in line with God's views of Christian stewardship?*

_____

_____

_____

_____

_____

_____

_____

_____

Prosperity knits a man to the World. He feels that is "finding his place in it," while really it is finding its place in him.

C. S. LEWIS

HEALTH

An Introduction

> Do not be fooled: You cannot cheat God. People harvest only what they plant.
>
> GALATIANS 6:7 NCV

what really counts

Every day, you make many decisions that affect your long-term health. What you eat, drink, and breathe today may impact your life in more ways than you thought possible. When you want to be used by God, you have to be in good enough shape to serve Him. If you don't feel good physically because you're not taking care of yourself, it can affect your mental and emotional state in negative ways.

Take a look at your schedule—are you allowing your body enough rest? Your body was designed to have a day off every week, so that you can refresh and recharge. How do you feel about your food choices? A little junk food in moderation won't kill you, but you'll feel the impact of your diet someday. Your biggest tests often come on the weekends—are you going to say no to those things that are really harmful for you, like alcohol, drugs, and casual sex?

You may think you're squeezing by, but some addictions and diseases you might pick up now won't show up until a few decades later. One day, you may want to start a family and find out that you picked up something in your teens that's harmed your system permanently. It all comes from the law of sowing and reaping—you'll reap what you sow, you'll reap later than you sow, and you'll reap more than you sow. It's up to you to make sure you'll want to harvest that crop when the time comes.

> Joy and Temperance and Repose slam the door on the doctor's nose.
>
> HENRY WADSWORTH LONGFELLOW

Health
Body and Soul

You created my inmost being; you knit me together in my mother's womb. I praise you because I am fearfully and wonderfully made.

PSALM 139:13–14 NIV

what really counts

You're young. You want to look good. You feel you have plenty of years ahead of you to take better care of yourself. What's the big deal about skipping a few meals every now and then, or living off junk food? Everybody else seems to be, so why shouldn't you? There are plenty of reasons why now's the time to start loving the one body God gave you. Your life is not one short sprint that you burst through quickly; it's more like a long-distance marathon. You want to train for the finish line that you can't even see yet. When an athlete trains for a cross-country event, she focuses on building her stamina so she won't burn out. The coach can't see what she eats before the race, but if she's skipped breakfast or wolfed down a candy bar, those last few miles are going to be tough.

It's the same for you. The habits you develop now can be impossible to break as you move into your twenties and thirties. Every day teens begin developing the foundations of major disease, and some even die. A high-stress lifestyle packed with the desire to be attractive on the outside can lead to some poor decision making. Problems such as anorexia and bulimia are rampant among the teen population, and they can wreak havoc on your long-term health. Athletes may succumb to the desire to pump up with steroids. And drugs and alcohol may make you think you look cool, but they can lead to lifetime addictions, not to mention other tragedies.

Why not start taking care of yourself now? Paul said your body is a temple of the Holy Spirit. "You are not your own; you were bought at a price. Therefore honor God with your body" (1 Corinthians 6:19–20 NIV). Try to make at least one good choice a day for your body. Instead of grabbing your usual burger and fries in the cafeteria, grab a baked potato and something your grandma might serve you. Take a break from staring at the computer screen in the afternoon and go walk around outside. You'll find that your mental outlook on life is related to your physical well-being a lot more than you think. Like the runner in training for a long-distance event, your body will perform its best when you treat it with care.

Health
Body and Soul

What Matters Most...

- Honoring God with the one body He gave you.

- Putting only good things into your body.

- Staying clear of things and people that can pollute your mind and body.

- Praying that God will give you the self-control you need to take care of yourself.

- Thinking of the long-term implications of the choices you make today.

What Doesn't Matter...

- What everybody else is doing. Honor God with your body, even when you feel alone.

- What gorgeous people look like on the covers of magazines. False outer images can hide hidden diseases of abuse.

- What you see in the mirror. Your true self-worth should come from a reflection of God's Word.

- Comparing your looks to other people's. God chose your body, and it is perfect to Him.

- What feels good now. Think of your whole life ahead of you and try to maximize those years to come.

Focus Points...

No discipline seems pleasant at the time, but painful. Later on, however, it produces a harvest of righteousness and peace for those who have been trained by it.
HEBREWS 12:11 NIV

A joyful heart is good medicine, but a broken spirit dries up the bones.
PROVERBS 17:22 NASB

Dear friends, God is good. So I beg you to offer your bodies to him as a living sacrifice, pure and pleasing.
ROMANS 12:1 CEV

He heals the brokenhearted and binds up their wounds.
PSALM 147:3 NIV

what really counts

My dear friend ... I pray that you are doing well in every way and that your health is good.
3 JOHN 2 NCV

It is the part of a Christian to take care of his own body for the very purpose that by its soundness and wellbeing he may be enabled to labor ... for the aid of those who are in want.

MARTIN LUTHER

The human body seems indestructible when we are young. However, it is incredibly fragile and must be cared for if it is to serve us for a lifetime.

JAMES DOBSON

Health
Sabbath Rest

> Anyone who enters God's rest will rest from his work as God did.
>
> HEBREWS 4:10 NCV

It always happens at the worst time—you open your cell phone to make a call, but nothing happens. The battery is dead. The phone is worthless to you then; it is nothing more than a highly styled piece of plastic. There's no way you can bang it or make it work without plugging it back into the charger. Your body is no different. When you wear yourself out without pausing to recharge your batteries, you may become useless as well.

Everyone needs to take a break one day a week to rest and refuel. God gave you the example to follow when He declared the Sabbath a day to catch up on rest. He clearly commanded, "Six days you shall labor and do all your work, but the seventh day is a Sabbath to the LORD your God. On it you shall not do any work" (Exodus 20:9–10 NIV). It's not as easy as it sounds, though. As a student, you may feel there's no way you'll be able to take a break and still finish everything you have to do.

314

But when you start seeing Sundays as the one day when you'll relax and rejuvenate, it makes you look at your schedule differently. Maybe you could find a few extra hours to study during the week to make up for the lost time on Sunday. You don't have to be legalistic about it; Jesus performed miracles on Sunday. Church pastors and other administrators usually take Mondays off, since Sunday is a busy workday for them. But as much as possible, try to see the Sabbath as a separate, holy day set aside for you to refresh your soul and worship.

Can you imagine what a piece of music would sound like if there were no rests? It would be only a constant tone—it wouldn't be at all pleasing to the ear. Your life is like the greatest symphony ever composed, and God is directing it. He loves to see you busy at times, working hard, and accomplishing the tasks you've been given. But it's also beautiful for Him to see you rest and repose—maybe that means throwing a football around the backyard with your little brother, or sitting outside under a tree noticing how cool the cloud formations are. Often, when you take a moment to rest, it gives you a chance to remember and appreciate how much God has done for you.

Health
Sabbath Rest

What Matters Most...

◎ Honoring God by recognizing the Sabbath as a special day of rest.

◎ Realizing your body needs to pause, in the same way music needs rests.

◎ Finding ways to relax creatively and enjoy the fellowship of your friends and family.

◎ Enjoying the Sabbath as a gift from God and thanking Him for it.

◎ Learning to use your time more efficiently throughout the week, so that you won't have to play catch-up on Sunday.

What **Doesn't** Matter...

◎ Being legalistic and judging others who work on Sunday.

◎ Starting a new tradition, even though you don't normally rest on the Sabbath.

◎ Comparing your Sundays to everyone else's.

◎ Giving up those hours that you could be getting more done.

◎ Feeling lazy when you don't study or work one day—you need the break!

Focus Points...

Those who receive that rest which God promised will rest from their own work, just as God rested from his.
HEBREWS 4:10 GNT

If you treat the Sabbath as a day of joy, GOD's holy day as a celebration ... then you'll be free to enjoy GOD!
ISAIAH 58:13–14 MSG

Six days you shall gather it, but on the seventh day, the Sabbath, there will be none.
EXODUS 16:26 NKJV

My soul finds rest in God alone; my salvation comes from him.
PSALM 62:1 NIV

If you are tired from carrying heavy burdens, come to me and I will give you rest.
MATTHEW 11:28 CEV

We benefit by that discipline of protecting our day of rest and worship. It's like shutting down the machine for oiling. We work more efficiently.

ROGER PALMS

Rhythm is at the literal core of all that exists. And for human beings, this rhythm of life requires rest.

MARK NICHOLAS

What Matters Most to Me About
Health

God gave you a body, mind, and soul—yet when you do not take care of each of these areas, you're not complete. You can't learn and grow spiritually if your body is falling apart.

◎ *When is the last time you had a checkup? Do you think you're in good shape?*

_____

_____

_____

_____

_____

what really counts _____

_____

_____

◎ *Are there any areas where you feel you might need to be more careful, such as your nutrition, exercise, weekend activities, or rest?*

_____

_____

_____

_____

_____

_____

_____

◉ *Write down three steps you want to take this week to start improving in those areas.*

_____

_____

_____

_____

_____

_____

_____

_____

_____

◉ *From those steps, develop a list of long-term goals you'd like to accomplish with your health. Share these goals with someone you care about, and ask him or her to hold you accountable.*

_____

_____

_____

_____

_____

_____

_____

_____

_____

Our religious activities should be ordered in such a way as to have plenty of time for the cultivation of the fruits of solitude and silence.

A. W. TOZER